Scala Puzzlers

Scala Puzzlers

Andrew Phillips, Nermin Šerifović

artima

ARTIMA PRESS
WALNUT CREEK, CALIFORNIA

Scala Puzzlers
First Edition

Andrew Phillips and Nermin Šerifović are Scala aficionados who co-maintain the
Scala Puzzlers website, scalapuzzlers.com.

Artima Press is an imprint of Artima, Inc.
2070 N Broadway #305, Walnut Creek, California 94597

First edition published as PrePrint™ eBook 2014
First edition published 2014
Build date of this impression November 25, 2014
Produced in the United States of America

18 17 16 15 14   1 2 3 4 5

ISBN-10: 0-9815316-7-9
ISBN-13: 978-0-9815316-7-0

Library of Congress Control Number: 2014936641

The cover contains a depiction of the *Penrose stairs*, an "impossible staircase"
created by Lionel and Roger Penrose.

To my mother Karin, a trickle of whose wonderful writing ability has hopefully made its way into this book, my patient, `scalac`-wrestling girlfriend Libby, and Bill Venners, without whom the two of us would not have met - A.P.

To my wonderful wife Džana, for her unreserved support and putting up with yet another side project of mine. To my amazing boys, Immy and Rayan, who were curious if I had been writing a "real" book, one that starts with "Once upon a time" and ends with "The End". To my loving parents, Nađa and Sabrija, who devoted much of their lives to their children's education. - N.Š.

Overview

Contents

Contents

Contents

Foreword

Puzzles are fun. I still remember the first time I came across the "puzzler" format for a programming language. It was when Neal Gafter presented the latest Java puzzlers to me that he and Josh Bloch had collected. At the time, Neal was maintaining the `javac` compiler that I had written. The puzzles were hard! I guessed wrong quite a few times, to Neal's delight.

I am pleased that there is now a book that continues the puzzler tradition in Scala. The book presents thirty-six puzzles arising from surprising effects, interactions of features, or consequences of encodings that are not obvious at the surface. The puzzles were collected over some years with extensive input from the Scala community.

Andrew and Nermin distill each puzzler to its essence and make it easily understandable. After having had the pleasure to try to pick the right solution among a set of choices, you are then led to the why: What are the reasons for the perhaps surprising solution? It is here that the book really shines, because it provides clear explanations of the underlying principles that lead to the observed program behavior. What I liked particularly about the book is that the explanations often lead to new insights. They tell you not just anecdotes of surprising behavior but something deep about how Scala is put together. In that way, the puzzles will help you develop a more profound understanding of the language.

I hope you have as much fun reading the book and trying to solve the puzzles as I had. And, if you must know, yes, there were some puzzles I could not solve.

Martin Odersky
Somewhere over the Atlantic
May 26, 2014

Preface

When you start getting into a new programming language, much is initially confusing simply due to lack of knowledge of the language. As your experience and ability to reason about the language grows, head-scratching moments related purely to the language tend to be replaced by system-level problems such as dependency conflicts or hard-to-reproduce race conditions.

One of things we really liked about Josh Bloch and Neal Gafter's *Java Puzzlers* is that it allowed us to reengage with Java outside the context of deadlines and day jobs. The puzzlers not only triggered our problem-solving itch. They helped us correct and deepen our understanding of the language.

Soon after we started learning Scala, we thought it would be really useful to collect a similar set of puzzlers—one, in the spirit of the times, built and maintained by the community. Thus, scalapuzzlers.com was born.

Encouraged by the positive feedback we received, we decided to collect and expand the puzzlers into this book. Our goal has been to explain the puzzlers' behavior in much greater detail and discuss potential implications and possible workarounds. We have strived to treat each puzzler as an opportunity to showcase an unusual part of the language, or highlight aspects of a common language feature that are not so well-known.

Researching and explaining each of the puzzlers in detail has been a lot of fun and a great learning experience. We hope you'll get as much out of this book, both in terms of knowledge and of enjoyment, as we have.

And lastly, if you come across a puzzling piece of Scala code, please submit it to us at scalapuzzlers.com. We'd love to have you join the puzzler community!

Andrew Phillips, Nermin Šerifović
Boston, Massachusetts
May 28, 2014

Acknowledgments

We are indebted to everyone who has been involved in making this book and scalapuzzlers.com happen, whether by providing the original sources for puzzlers, through comments or suggestions, or simply by spreading the word.

Sincere thanks go to our editors Jessica Kerr, Bill Venners and Theresa Gonzalez for their probing and thoughtful reviews, and to Darlene Wallach and George Berger for their help in layout and adapting the publishing system to handle the puzzlers.

We would especially like to thank all contributors to scalapuzzlers.com: Dominik Gruntz, A. P. Marki, Simon Schäfer, Konstantine Golikov, Seth Tisue, Daniel C. Sobral, Luc Bourlier, Vassil Dichev and Andraž Bajt. Your submissions have provided the basis and inspiration for this book.

We would also like to express our gratitude to the following readers who spotted errors or suggested improvements: Cay Horstmann, Harish Hurchurn, Marcin Kubala, Edward G Prentice, Alex Varju and, in particular, Dominik Gruntz, for his thorough review and the many useful suggestions he contributed.

Introduction

Getting code to do what we want it to do is perhaps the essence of our purpose as developers. So there are few things more intriguing or important than a piece of code that we *think* we understand, but that behaves contrary to our expectations.

This book is a collection of such examples in Scala. It is not only an entertaining and instructive way of understanding this highly expressive language better. It will also help you recognize many counter-intuitive traps and pitfalls and prevent them from biting you in production.

How to read this book

The puzzlers in this book are not listed in any specific order. You should be able to open the book at a random puzzler just as easily as reading it from cover to cover.

If you find a specific area of the Scala language interesting and are looking for related puzzlers, the Subject Index at the end of this book is for you. There, we have tried to catalog the puzzlers according to the subject(s) they explore.

All code samples presented in the puzzlers are intended to be interpreted as statements that will be run inside a clean, 2.11 Scala REPL.[1] Where recent language changes such as deprecations have resulted in slightly different behavior with respect to 2.10.x Scala versions, we have added explanatory comments or footnotes.

Although this book has been heavily reviewed, errors will inevitably slip through. If you find an error, please report it on the errata page for this book: http://booksites.artima.com/scala_puzzlers/errata.

---

[1] Start the REPL (Read-Evaluate-Print-Loop) by typing "scala" on the command line.

EBook features

This book is available in both paper and PDF eBook form. The eBook is not simply an electronic copy of the paper version of the book. While the content is the same as in the paper version, the eBook has been carefully designed and optimized for reading on a computer screen.

The first thing to notice is that most references within the eBook are hyperlinked. If you select a reference to a chapter, figure, or glossary entry, your PDF viewer should take you immediately to the selected item so that you do not have to flip around to find it.

Additionally, at the bottom of each page in the eBook are a number of navigation links. The "Cover," "Overview," and "Contents" links take you to the front matter of the book. The "Index" link takes you to the index in the back of the book. Finally, the "Discuss" link takes you to an online forum where you discuss questions with other readers, the authors, and the larger Scala community. If you find a typo, or something you think could be explained better, please click on the "Suggest" link, which will take you to an online web application where you can give the authors feedback.

Although the same pages appear in the eBook as the printed book, blank pages are removed and the remaining pages renumbered. The pages are numbered differently so that it is easier for you to determine PDF page numbers when printing only a portion of the eBook. The pages in the eBook are, therefore, numbered exactly as your PDF viewer will number them.

Typographic conventions

The first time a *term* is used, it is italicized. Small code examples, such as x + 1, are written inline with a mono-spaced font. Larger code examples are put into mono-spaced quotation blocks like this:

```
def hello() {
    println("Hello, world!")
}
```

When interactive shells are shown, responses from the shell are shown in a lighter font:

```
scala> 3 + 4
res0: Int = 7
```

Scala Puzzlers

Puzzler 1

Hi There!

Scala places a strong emphasis on writing simple, concise code. Its syntax for anonymous functions, `arg => expr`, makes it easy to construct function literals with minimal boilerplate, even when the functions consist of multiple statements.

For functions with self-explanatory parameters, you can do better and use placeholder syntax. This trims away the parameter declaration. For example:

```
List(1, 2).map { i => i + 1 }
```

becomes:

```
List(1, 2).map { _ + 1 }
```

The following two statements are equivalent:

```
scala> List(1, 2).map { i => i + 1 }
res1: List[Int] = List(2, 3)
scala> List(1, 2).map { _ + 1 }
res0: List[Int] = List(2, 3)
```

What if you added a debugging statement to the above example to help you understand when the function is applied? What is the result of executing the following code in the REPL?

```
List(1, 2).map { i => println("Hi"); i + 1 }
List(1, 2).map { println("Hi"); _ + 1 }
```

Possibilities

1. Prints:

```
Hi
List[Int] = List(2, 3)
Hi
List[Int] = List(2, 3)
```

2. Prints:

```
Hi
Hi
List[Int] = List(2, 3)
Hi
Hi
List[Int] = List(2, 3)
```

3. Prints:

```
Hi
Hi
List[Int] = List(2, 3)
Hi
List[Int] = List(2, 3)
```

4. The first statement prints:

```
Hi
Hi
List[Int] = List(2, 3)
```

and the second fails to compile.

Explanation

You need not be concerned with compiler errors, because the code compiles without problems; yet, it does not behave the way you might expect. The correct answer is number 3:

```scala
scala> List(1, 2).map { i => println("Hi"); i + 1 }
Hi
Hi
res23: List[Int] = List(2, 3)

scala> List(1, 2).map { println("Hi"); _ + 1 }
Hi
res25: List[Int] = List(2, 3)
```

What is going on here? If the function with the explicit argument prints Hi twice, as it is invoked for each element in the list, why doesn't our function with placeholder syntax do the same?

Since anonymous functions are often passed as arguments, it's common to see them surrounded by { ... } in code. It's easy to think that these curly braces represent an anonymous function, but instead they delimit a *block expression*: one or multiple statements, with the last determining the result of the block.

The way the two code blocks are parsed determines the difference in behavior. The first statement, { i => println("Hi"); i + 1 }, is identified as *one* function literal expression of the form arg => expr, with expr here being the block, println("Hi"); i + 1. Since the println statement is part of the function body, it is executed each time the function is invoked.

```scala
scala> val printAndAddOne =
         (i: Int) => { println("Hi"); i + 1 }
printAndAddOne: Int => Int = <function1>

scala> List(1, 2).map(printAndAddOne)
Hi
Hi
res29: List[Int] = List(2, 3)
```

In the second statement, however, the code block is identified as *two* expressions: println("Hi") and _ + 1. The block is executed, and the last expression (which is conveniently of the required function type, Int => Int) is passed to map. The println statement is not part of the function body. It is invoked when the argument to map is *evaluated*, not as part of the execution of map.

```scala
scala> val printAndReturnAFunc =
         { println("Hi"); (_: Int) + 1 }
Hi
printAndReturnAFunc: Int => Int = <function1>

scala> List(1, 2).map(printAndReturnAFunc)
res30: List[Int] = List(2, 3)
```

Discussion

The key lesson here is that the scope of an anonymous function defined using placeholder syntax stretches *only* to the expression containing the underscore (_). This differs from a "regular" anonymous function, whose body contains everything from the rocket symbol (=>) to the end of the code block. Here's an example:

```scala
scala> val regularFunc =
         { a: Any => println("foo"); println(a); "baz" }
regularFunc: Any => String = <function1>

scala> regularFunc("hello")
foo
hello
res42: String = baz
```

It's as though a function with placeholder syntax is "confined" to its own code block. For example, the following two functions are equivalent:

```scala
scala> val anonymousFunc =
         { println("foo"); println(_: Any); "baz" }
foo
anonymousFunc: String = baz
```

```
scala> val confinedFunc =
         { println("foo"); { a: Any => println(a) }; "baz" }
foo
confinedFunc: String = baz
```

 Scala encourages concise code, but there is such a thing as *too* much conciseness. When using placeholder syntax, be aware of the scope of the function that is created.

Puzzler 2

UPSTAIRS downstairs

Scala offers several convenient ways to initialize multiple variables. Sometimes, this can lead to unexpected surprises.

What is the result of executing the following code in the REPL?

```
var MONTH = 12; var DAY = 24
var (HOUR, MINUTE, SECOND) = (12, 0, 0)
```

Possibilities

1. Prints:

   ```
   MONTH: Int = 12
   DAY: Int = 24
   HOUR: Int = 12
   MINUTE: Int = 0
   SECOND: Int = 0
   ```

2. Both statements fail to compile.

3. The first statement prints:

   ```
   MONTH: Int = 12
   DAY: Int = 24
   ```

   and the second throws a runtime exception.

4. The first statement prints:

```
MONTH: Int = 12
DAY: Int = 24
```

and the second fails to compile.

Explanation

You might recall something about uppercase variables and constant values and wonder whether either line compiles. As it happens, the first line compiles fine; it's the second statement that fails to compile. The correct answer is number 4:

```
scala> var MONTH = 12; var DAY = 24
MONTH: Int = 12
DAY: Int = 24

scala> var (HOUR, MINUTE, SECOND) = (12, 0, 0)
<console>:11: error: not found: value HOUR
       var (HOUR, MINUTE, SECOND) = (12, 0, 0)
            ^

<console>:11: error: not found: value MINUTE
       var (HOUR, MINUTE, SECOND) = (12, 0, 0)
                  ^

<console>:11: error: not found: value SECOND
       var (HOUR, MINUTE, SECOND) = (12, 0, 0)
```

Scala will happily allow you to use an uppercase variable name for plain, single-value assignments of vals and vars, as in the case of MONTH and DAY. However, as the second statement demonstrates, uppercase variable names are tricky in multiple-variable assignments.

This trickiness arises because multiple-variable assignments are based on pattern matching, and within a pattern match, variables starting with an uppercase letter take on a special meaning: they are *stable identifiers*.

Stable identifiers are intended for matching against constants:

```
scala> final val TheAnswer = 42
scala> def checkGuess(guess: Int) = guess match {
         case TheAnswer => "Your guess is correct"
         case _ => "Try again"
       }
scala> checkGuess(21)
res8: String = Try again
scala> checkGuess(42)
res9: String = Your guess is correct
```

Lowercase variables, by contrast, define *variable patterns*, which cause values to be assigned:

```
scala> var (hour, minute, second) = (12, 0, 0)
hour: Int = 12
minute: Int = 0
second: Int = 0
```

In the case of our code example, you are not carrying out a variable assignment as intended, therefore, but a match against constant values.

Discussion

If you are trying to use uppercase variable names that, by extreme coincidence, happen to match values that are in scope (which could happen with common names in a large program), the pattern match will compile successfully, and either succeed or fail depending on whether the values match:

```
val HOUR = 12; val MINUTE, SECOND = 0;
scala> var (HOUR, MINUTE, SECOND) = (12, 0, 0)
val HOUR = 13; val MINUTE, SECOND = 0;
scala> var (HOUR, MINUTE, SECOND) = (12, 0, 0)
scala.MatchError: (12,0,0) (of class scala.Tuple3)
  ...
```

Note that, even in the first case where the match is successful, no variables are actually assigned: stable identifiers are never assigned a value during a pattern match, by definition. In short, at best nothing happens, otherwise you get an exception at runtime—neither of which was intended.

Lowercase variables can also be treated as stable identifiers by enclosing them in backticks. In that case, they must be vals, since we are treating them as constants.

```scala
final val theAnswer = 42
def checkGuess(guess: Int) = guess match {
  case `theAnswer` => "Your guess is correct"
  case _ => "Try again"
}
scala> checkGuess(42)
res0: String = Your guess is correct

var theAnswer: Int = 42 // not a val, and not final either

scala> def checkGuess(guess: Int) = guess match {
        case `theAnswer` => "Your guess is correct"
        case _ => "Try again"
      }
<console>:9: error: stable identifier required, but
  theAnswer found.
        case `theAnswer` => "Your guess is correct"
```

It's unlikely to come as a surprise that uppercase names for vars are not considered Scala best practice: use lowercase names for vars (better still, avoid them completely!), and uppercase names for constants. As described in *The Scala Language Specification*, constants should also be declared final.[1] This prevents subclasses from overriding them, and has an additional performance benefit in that the compiler can inline them.

 Use uppercase variable names only for constants.

---

[1] Odersky, *The Scala Language Specification*, Section 4.1. [Ode14]

Puzzler 3

Location, Location, Location

In many object-oriented languages, it is common to accept parameters in a class constructor for the purpose of assigning them to class members:

```
class MyClass(param1, param2, ...) {
  val member1 = param1
  val member2 = param2
  ...
}
```

Scala, which favors concise code, lets you avoid this redundancy by declaring members and constructor parameters in one go:

```
class MyClass(val member1, val member2, ...) {
  ...
}
```

What is the result of executing the following code?

```
trait A {
  val audience: String
  println("Hello " + audience)
}
class BMember(a: String = "World") extends A {
  val audience = a
  println("I repeat: Hello " + audience)
}
```

PUZZLER 3 · Location, Location, Location

```
class BConstructor(val audience: String = "World") extends A {
  println("I repeat: Hello " + audience)
}
new BMember("Readers")
new BConstructor("Readers")
```

Possibilities

1. Prints:

   ```
   Hello Readers
   I repeat: Hello Readers
   Hello Readers
   I repeat: Hello Readers
   ```

2. Prints:

   ```
   Hello World
   I repeat: Hello Readers
   Hello World
   I repeat: Hello Readers
   ```

3. Prints:

   ```
   Hello null
   I repeat: Hello Readers
   Hello Readers
   I repeat: Hello Readers
   ```

4. Prints:

   ```
   Hello null
   I repeat: Hello Readers
   Hello null
   I repeat: Hello Readers
   ```

Explanation

The key question here is when precisely the assignment of "Readers" to audience becomes visible. You may also wonder whether or how the default value, "World", is involved. Surely the small optimization of moving the member declaration of audience into the constructor parameter list has no impact, though? Not so—the correct answer is number 3:

```
scala> new BMember("Readers")
Hello null
I repeat: Hello Readers
res3: BMember = BMember@1aa6f6eb

scala> new BConstructor("Readers")
Hello Readers
I repeat: Hello Readers
res4: BConstructor = BConstructor@64b6603a
```

In other words, the value of audience in A differs if the member is declared in B's constructor parameters, as opposed to the constructor body.

To understand the difference between member declarations in the class body versus in the constructor parameter list, you need to examine Scala's class initialization sequence. Consider again the class declarations:

```
class BMember(a: String = "World") extends A {
  ...
}

class BConstructor(val audience: String = "World") extends A {
  ...
}
```

Both class declarations are of the form:[1]

```
class c(param1) extends superclass { statements }
```

According to the language specification,[2] the initialization sequence for new BMember("Readers") and new BConstructor("Readers") will be:

---

[1] Odersky, *The Scala Language Specification*, Section 5.3. [Ode14]
[2] Odersky, *The Scala Language Specification*, Section 5.1. [Ode14]

1. The argument "Readers" is evaluated. In this case, there is nothing to do here, but if the argument were specified as an expression (*e.g.*, "readers".capitalize), this would be evaluated first.

2. The class being constructed is initialized by evaluating the template:[3],[4]

   superclass { statements }

   a) First, the superclass constructor A
   b) Then the statement sequence in the body of the subclass, either BMember or BConstructor

Here, note that we are omitting details regarding traits, *etc.*, that do not apply to this example. In the case of BMember, "Readers" is assigned to the constructor parameter, a, in the first step. When A's constructor is invoked, audience is still uninitialized, so the default string value null is printed. "Readers" is assigned to audience, and then printed, only when the statement sequence in the body of BMember executes.

BConstructor's case is different: here "Readers" is evaluated *and assigned to audience straight away*, as part of the evaluation of the constructor arguments. The value of audience is already "Readers" by the time A's constructor is invoked.

Discussion

In general, the pattern in BConstructor is preferred as its behavior leaves less room for surprises. The val declared in the superclass never exists in an uninitialized state.

You can achieve the same result without declaring audience in the constructor parameter list by using an *early field definition*[5] clause. This allows you to perform additional computations on the constructor arguments (*e.g.*, normalizing the case of string arguments), or to create anonymous classes with correctly initialized values:

---

[3] Odersky, *The Scala Language Specification*, Section 5.1. [Ode14]

[4] A *template* is the body of a class, trait, or singleton object definition. It defines the type signature, behavior, and initial state of a class, trait, or object.

[5] Odersky, *The Scala Language Specification*, Section 5.1.6. [Ode14]

```scala
class BEarlyDef(a: String = "World") extends {
  val audience = a
} with A {
  println("I repeat: Hello " + audience)
}
scala> new BEarlyDef("Readers")
Hello Readers
I repeat: Hello Readers
res7: BEarlyDef = BEarlyDef@44c93da7

scala> new {
        val audience = "Readers"
      } with A {
        println("I repeat: Hello " + audience)
      }
Hello Readers
I repeat: Hello Readers
res0: A = anon1@71e16512
```

Early definitions define and assign member values *before* the supertype constructor is called. The initialization sequence, as per the sections of the language specification applicable in this case,[6] is:

> A class is initialized by evaluating the template:
>
> 1. First, early definitions in the order they are defined,
>
> 2. then, the superclass constructor,
>
> 3. finally, the statements in the default constructor.

In short, superclass and supertrait initialization code is executed *after* parameter evaluation and early field definitions and *before* the initialization statements of the class or trait being instantiated. The direct superclass and mixed-in traits are initialized in left-to-right order as they appear in the class, trait, or object definition.

An extended code sample puts all of this together:

---

[6]Odersky, *The Scala Language Specification*, Sections 5.1.1, 5.1, and 5.1.6. [Ode14]

```scala
trait A {
  val audience: String
  println("Hello " + audience)
}

trait AfterA {
  val introduction: String
  println(introduction)
}

class BEvery(val audience: String) extends {
  val introduction =
    { println("Evaluating early def"); "Are you there?" }
} with A with AfterA {
  println("I repeat: Hello " + audience)
}

scala> new BEvery({ println("Evaluating param"); "Readers" })
Evaluating param
Evaluating early def
Hello Readers
Are you there?
I repeat: Hello Readers
res3: BEvery = BEvery@6bcc2569
```

Think of superclass constructors and supertrait initializers as being inserted, in left-to-right order of declaration, after the opening bracket of the class or object body (which forms the primary constructor).

Puzzler 4

Now You See Me, Now You Don't

Scala supports object-oriented programming concepts, and inheritance is a prominent one. When working with inheritance, it is often useful to override default values set in parent classes and traits. Adding multiple levels of inheritance makes things more interesting, such as in the following program. What does it print?

```scala
trait A {
  val foo: Int
  val bar = 10
  println("In A: foo: " + foo + ", bar: " + bar)
}
class B extends A {
  val foo: Int = 25
  println("In B: foo: " + foo + ", bar: " + bar)
}
class C extends B {
  override val bar = 99
  println("In C: foo: " + foo + ", bar: " + bar)
}
new C()
```

Possibilities

1. Prints:

   ```
   In A: foo: 0, bar: 0
   In B: foo: 25, bar: 0
   In C: foo: 25, bar: 99
   ```

2. Prints:

   ```
   In A: foo: 0, bar: 10
   In B: foo: 25, bar: 10
   In C: foo: 25, bar: 99
   ```

3. Prints:

   ```
   In A: foo: 0, bar: 0
   In B: foo: 25, bar: 99
   In C: foo: 25, bar: 99
   ```

4. Prints:

   ```
   In A: foo: 25, bar: 99
   In B: foo: 25, bar: 99
   In C: foo: 25, bar: 99
   ```

Explanation

The correct answer is number 1. To understand why, you need to look into the details of the program execution.

First, you should remember that every Scala class has a primary constructor that is not explicitly defined, but interwoven with the class definition.[1] All statements in the class definition form the body of the primary constructor, and that includes field definitions (which is, by the way, the reason Scala does not intrinsically differentiate between class fields and values

---

[1]Odersky, *The Scala Language Specification*, Section 5.3. [Ode14]

local to the constructor). Hence, all the code in trait A and classes B and C belongs to the constructor body.

The following rules control the initialization and overriding behavior of vals:[2]

1. Superclasses are fully initialized before subclasses.

2. Members are initialized in the order they are declared.

3. When a val is overridden, it can still only be initialized once.

4. Like an abstract val, an overridden val will have a default initial value during the construction of superclasses.

Therefore, even though bar appears to have an initial value assigned in trait A and class B, that is not the case, because it is overridden in class C. This means that during the construction of trait A, bar has the default initial value of 0 and not the assigned value of 10. Essentially, initialization order gets in the way, and the assignment of 10 to bar in trait A is completely invisible because bar is overridden in class C, where it is initialized to 99. Similarly, the value foo, since it is assigned a non-default value in class B, has value 0 in A and then 25 in B and C.

This issue can manifest itself with abstract fields, when such a field is used after it is declared, but before it is certain to have been initialized in a subclass. Basically, all constructs that are initialized during class construction (including non-abstract fields) and depend on abstract fields are prone to initialization order problems.

Discussion

Scala inherits initialization order rules from Java. Java makes sure that superclasses are initialized first to allow safe use of superclass fields from the subclass constructors, guaranteeing that the fields will be properly initialized. Traits compile into interfaces and concrete (*i.e.*, non-abstract) classes, so the same rules apply.

---

[2]"Why is my abstract or overridden val null?" [Why]

Default initial values

For the record, Scala specifies default initial values as:

- 0 for Byte, Short, and Int
- OL, 0.0f, and 0.0d for Int, Long, Float, and Double, respectively
- '\0' for Char
- false for Boolean
- () for Unit
- null for all other types

You might wonder if the compiler could somehow warn you about abstract fields that are used before being initialized to non-default values.[3] Unfortunately, no warning about uninitialized values is given by default—only testing can catch them. However, there is an advanced compiler option that can be used to detect them:

-Xcheckinit Wrap field accessors to throw an exception on uninitialized accesses.

This option adds a wrapper around all potentially uninitialized field accesses, and throws an exception rather than using a default value. The addition of a runtime check to field accessors adds significant overhead, so it's not recommended that you use it in production code.

If you start the Scala REPL session with the –Xcheckinit flag, the following exception will be thrown upon executing **new** C():

```
scala> new C()
scala.UninitializedFieldError: Uninitialized field:
    <console>: 10
  at C.bar(<console>:10)
  at A$class.$init$(<console>:10)
  ...
```

---

[3]In the manner of the "X may be used uninitialized in this function" warning from the C compiler, for instance.

As a good practice, you may want to turn on this flag in your automated builds to spot such problems early.

Now that you are aware of the nature of the problem, is there something you can do about it? The following sections provide some workarounds.

Methods

One option is to declare bar as a def instead of a val, which in this case results in the behavior you expect:

```
trait A {
  val foo: Int
  def bar: Int = 10
  println("In A: foo: " + foo + ", bar: " + bar)
}
class B extends A {
  val foo: Int = 25
  println("In B: foo: " + foo + ", bar: " + bar)
}
class C extends B {
  override def bar: Int = 99
  println("In C: foo: " + foo + ", bar: " + bar)
}
scala> new C
In A: foo: 0, bar: 99
In B: foo: 25, bar: 99
In C: foo: 25, bar: 99
```

The reason defining bar as a def works here is that method bodies do not belong to the primary constructor and, therefore, take no part in class initialization. In addition, bar is overridden in C, and the polymorphic resolution selects that definition as the most specific one. Therefore, a call to bar in all three println statements invokes the overridden definition in class C.

One drawback of using methods is that they are evaluated upon each and every invocation. Also, Scala conforms to the Uniform Access Principle,[4] so defining a parameterless method in the superclass does not prevent it from

---

[4]Odersky, Spoon, Venners, *Programming in Scala*, Glossary online. [Odeb]

23

being overridden as a val in a subclass, which would cause the puzzling behavior to reappear, ruining all the careful planning.

Lazy vals

Another way to avoid such surprises is to declare bar as a *lazy val*. Lazy vals are initialized when accessed the first time. "Regular" vals, called *strict* or *eager*, are initialized when defined. Here's how that looks:

```scala
trait A {
  val foo: Int
  lazy val bar = 10
  println("In A: foo: " + foo + ", bar: " + bar)
}
class B extends A {
  val foo: Int = 25
  println("In B: foo: " + foo + ", bar: " + bar)
}
class C extends B {
  override lazy val bar = 99
  println("In C: foo: " + foo + ", bar: " + bar)
}
new C()
```

This program also works as expected:

```
In A: foo: 0, bar: 99
In B: foo: 25, bar: 99
In C: foo: 25, bar: 99
```

Declaring bar as a lazy val means it will be initialized to 99 during the construction of trait A, since that is where it is accessed for the first time. Lazy vals are initialized using compiler-generated methods, and here, the overridden version in trait C is the one that is called.

Note that lazy vals are typically used to defer expensive initializations to the last possible moment (sometimes they may never be initialized). That is not the goal here: in this case, lazy vals are used to ensure the proper order of initialization at runtime.

Be aware, however, that lazy vals can have some disadvantages:

1. They incur a slight performance cost, due to synchronization that happens under the hood.

2. You cannot declare an abstract lazy val.

3. Using lazy vals is prone to creating cyclic references that can result in stack overflow errors on first access, or possibly even deadlock.

4. You can even get a deadlock when a cyclic dependency does not exist between lazy vals, but between objects that declare them. Such scenarios can be very subtle and non-obvious.[5]

Pre-initialized fields

The same effect can also be achieved by using *pre-initialized fields* (also known as *early initializers*):

```
trait A {
  val foo: Int
  val bar = 10
  println("In A: foo: " + foo + ", bar: " + bar)
}

class B extends A {
  val foo: Int = 25
  println("In B: foo: " + foo + ", bar: " + bar)
}


class C extends {
  override val bar = 99
} with B {
  println("In C: foo: " + foo + ", bar: " + bar)
}
scala> new C
In A: foo: 0, bar: 99
In B: foo: 25, bar: 99
In C: foo: 25, bar: 99
```

---

[5] SIP-20, *Improved Lazy Vals Initialization* aims to significantly reduce the possibility of deadlocks by re-implementing the initialization mechanism.

The only difference between this and the original program is that `bar` is initialized in the early field definition clause of class C. An *early field definition* clause is the code within curly braces immediately following the `extends` keyword.[6] It is the part of a subclass that is intended to run before its superclass constructor.[7] By doing that, you make sure `bar` is initialized before trait A is constructed.

The best way to address potential initialization order problems depends on your use case. If evaluating expressions upon each access is not too expensive, you might reach for method definitions. Or, lazy `val`s might turn out to be the simplest solution for the users of your class so long as you avoid any circular dependencies. Otherwise, assuming you can make it clear to users that they should use early field definitions, plain old abstract `val`s can be a good choice.

---

[6]Odersky, *The Scala Language Specification*, Section 5.1.6. [Ode14]
[7]See Puzzler 3 for a more in-depth discussion of initialization order.

Puzzler 5

The Missing List

Scala's rich collections library provides many functions and operations on many different collection types. Sometimes, though, you may want to add your own "utility" operations.

This example represents an attempt (suboptimal, but more on that later) to sum the sizes of multiple collection instances. For example, the sum of the sizes of Vector("a"), List("b", "c"), and Array("d", "e", "f") should be $1 + 2 + 3 = 6$:

```
scala> sumSizes(Seq(Vector("a"), List("b", "c"),
        Array("d", "e", "f")))
res4: Int = 6
```

You may try to make such utility functions work on base collection types, such as Iterable, to ensure they are widely applicable. Obviously, the intention is that the operation behave in the same way regardless of the concrete collections passed in.

What is the result of executing the following code?

```
def sumSizes(collections: Iterable[Iterable[_]]): Int =
  collections.map(_.size).sum

sumSizes(List(Set(1, 2), List(3, 4)))
sumSizes(Set(List(1, 2), Set(3, 4)))
```

27

Possibilities

1. Prints:

   ```
   Int = 4
   Int = 4
   ```

2. Prints:

   ```
   Int = 4
   Int = 2
   ```

3. Prints:

   ```
   Int = 2
   Int = 4
   ```

4. Prints:

   ```
   Int = 2
   Int = 2
   ```

Explanation

You may wonder whether sumSizes is somehow counting the *number* of collections rather than their *sizes*, which would cause both statements to print 2, as in answer 4. As it happens, though, the correct answer is number 2:

```
scala> sumSizes(List(Set(1, 2), List(3, 4)))
res5: Int = 4

scala> sumSizes(Set(List(1, 2), Set(3, 4)))
res6: Int = 2
```

To understand what is going on, you need to recall another feature of the Scala collections library: its operations generally preserve the input collection type!

Developers coming from a Java background might expect that transforming an `Iterable` would produce a result that conforms to the `Iterable` interface, but could be any underlying implementation type. The Scala collections go one step further, though, and return an `Iterable` with the same type as the input type.[1]

This means the result type of the following statement *is also a set* and thus cannot contain multiple instances of the same item:

```
Set(List(1, 2), Set(3, 4)).map(_.size)
```

As a result, this intermediate value contains only one element:

```
scala> Set(List(1, 2), Set(3, 4)).map(_.size)
res7: scala.collection.immutable.Set[Int] = Set(2)
```

This behavior of sets explains the observed result.

Adding to the puzzlement here is the fact that `Set` does not appear anywhere in the type declaration of `sumSizes`. There is no obvious warning flag to make either the author or caller of the function think about the potential impact of the uniqueness constraint of `Set`s, or indeed other constraints with similar unintended consequences of other subtypes of `Iterable`.

Discussion

How can you avoid such surprises? One possible choice in this case would be to convert the outer collection to a known type, *e.g.*, using `toSeq`:

```
def sumSizes(collections: Iterable[Iterable[_]]): Int =
  collections.toSeq.map(_.size).sum

scala> sumSizes(List(Set(1, 2), List(3, 4)))
res0: Int = 4

scala> sumSizes(Set(List(1, 2), Set(3, 4)))
res1: Int = 4
```

---

[1] See the Scaladoc for `CanBuildFrom`. [EPF]

In this particular case, you can do even better. By switching to an implementation using fold, you can avoid the problem *and* eliminate one of the iterations through the outer collection:

```scala
def sumSizes(collections: Iterable[Iterable[_]]): Int =
  collections.foldLeft(0) {
    (sumOfSizes, collection) => sumOfSizes + collection.size
}
scala> sumSizes(List(Set(1, 2), List(3, 4)))
res8: Int = 4

scala> sumSizes(Set(List(1, 2), Set(3, 4)))
res9: Int = 4
```

Pay close attention to the possible input types to your methods that operate on collections. If you do not need to preserve the input type, consider constructing your own intermediate types with known characteristics.

Puzzler 6

Arg Arrgh!

Scala's concise syntax and rich set of functional primitives allow you to write powerful one-liners. The complexity of these statements can, however, make it difficult to understand the overall intention, at which point declaring a suitably named helper method is often a good idea.

For instance, assume you need to determine the result of applying a simple "generator" function, f, to an initial value, arg, multiple times. This can be achieved neatly using fold—a natural choice for recursive computations:

```
// n applications of f to arg: f(f(...f(arg)))
val result = (1 to n).foldLeft(arg) { (acc, _) => f(acc) }
```

This is certainly a concise solution to your problem, but figuring out what exactly this line does will generally require more than a quick glance.

You might attempt to make this line easier to understand by extracting it into a helper function, of which we'll consider a version with a single parameter list, applyNMulti, and a curried version, applyNCurried. You could then apply these helper functions to two generator functions: a simple one, nextInt, which applies only to Ints, and a more generic version, nextNumber, which uses the typeclass pattern[1] to handle all numeric types.

What is the result of executing the following code in the REPL?

```
def applyNMulti[T](n: Int)(arg: T, f: T => T) =
  (1 to n).foldLeft(arg) { (acc, _) => f(acc) }

def applyNCurried[T](n: Int)(arg: T)(f: T => T) =
  (1 to n).foldLeft(arg) { (acc, _) => f(acc) }
```

---

[1] Sobral, "Implicit tricks – the Type Class pattern." [Sob10]

```
def nextInt(n: Int) = n * n + 1

def nextNumber[N](n: N)(implicit numericOps: Numeric[N]) =
  numericOps.plus(numericOps.times(n, n), numericOps.one)

println(applyNMulti(3)(2, nextInt))
println(applyNCurried(3)(2)(nextInt))
println(applyNMulti(3)(2.0, nextNumber))
println(applyNCurried(3)(2.0)(nextNumber))
```

Possibilities

1. The first, second, and fourth statements print:

   ```
   677
   677
   677.0
   ```

   and the third fails to compile.

2. The first and second statements print:

   ```
   677
   677
   ```

   and the third and fourth fail to compile.

3. The first, second, and third statements print:

   ```
   677
   677
   677.0
   ```

   and the fourth fails to compile.

4. Prints:

   ```
   677
   677
   677.0
   677.0
   ```

Explanation

Using the simple nextInt generator function works fine, so what could go wrong in the generic case? The required numeric operations for Double are in scope, as you can verify:

```
scala> val doubleOps = implicitly[Numeric[Double]]
doubleOps: Numeric[Double] =
  scala.math.Numeric$DoubleIsFractional$@7c54c0ca
```

Perhaps the compiler simply does not like our generic version? Surely, though, both the third and fourth statements should then fail?

As it happens, this is not quite the case. Only the application of the *uncurried* version to the generic function, nextNumber, troubles the compiler, so the correct answer is number 1:

```
scala> println(applyNMulti(3)(2, nextInt))
677
```

```
scala> println(applyNCurried(3)(2)(nextInt))
677
```

```
scala> println(applyNMulti(3)(2.0, nextNumber))
<console>:10: error: could not find implicit value for
  parameter numericOps: Numeric[N]
            println(applyNMulti(3)(2.0, nextNumber))
                                  ^
```

```
scala> println(applyNCurried(3)(2.0)(nextNumber))
677.0
```

What is the compiler complaining about? The error message implies that the compiler is not looking for implicit evidence of type Numeric[Double], as you might expect, but for a Numeric[N]...?

Isn't N bound to Double by the use of 2.0 as the first argument, though? Yes, it is, but the key point here is that this does not help the compiler. The compiler attempts to satisfy the type requirements for each parameter in a parameter list *individually*, and is therefore not able to use information about a generic type provided by other arguments in the same parameter list.

In this case, the fact that the generic type N is bound to a specific type, Double, is not available when the compiler searches for the appropriate

33

numericOps. This is true even though the parameter that binds N appears before nextNumber in the parameter list!

In the curried case, on the other hand, N has been bound to Double as part of the evaluation of the *previous* parameter list, as opposed to an earlier parameter in the *same* list. The partially applied function to which nextNumber is applied indeed expects a Double, as demonstrated by its type signature:

```
scala> applyNCurried(3)(2.0) _
res9: (Double => Double) => Double = <function1>
```

Because the compiler knows that N is bound to Double when nextNumber is processed, it can find the appropriate implicit Numeric[Double] value in scope, allowing this variant to execute successfully.

Incidentally, this "type information propagation" is one of the reasons why so many of Scala's standard functions have curried definitions.

Discussion

You can make the uncurried variant succeed by explicitly specifying the type:

```
scala> println(applyNMulti(3)(2.0, nextNumber[Double]))
677.0
```

```
scala> println(applyNMulti[Double](3)(2.0, nextNumber))
677.0
```

This feels unnecessary, though, since the argument, 2.0, carries the type information. It is also not a practical solution if the initial value is passed as a variable rather than specified as a constant, since a change of the variable's type (*e.g.*, from Double to Float) will cause a compiler error that you should be able to avoid:

```
val firstVal = 2.0
```

```
scala> println(applyNMulti(3)(firstVal, nextNumber[Double]))
677.0
```

```
// refactored to use a Float
val firstVal = 2.0f
```

```
scala> println(applyNMulti(3)(firstVal, nextNumber[Double]))
<console>:11: error: type mismatch;
 found    : Double => Double
 required: AnyVal => AnyVal
    println(applyNMulti(3)(firstVal, nextNumber[Double]))
                                                  ^
```

Also, note that the typeclass pattern involving Numeric is not fundamental to this problem: any type constraint, such as a type bound, can cause the same behavior. As before, the curried version works as expected:

```
def nextAnyVal[N <: AnyVal](n: N) = n

scala> applyNCurried(3)(2.0)(nextAnyVal)
res21: Double = 2.0

scala> applyNMulti(3)(2.0, nextAnyVal)
<console>:10: error: type mismatch;
 found    : Nothing => Nothing
 required: Double => Double
              applyNMulti(3)(2.0, nextAnyVal)
                                  ^
```

Information about a type parameter is available only to *subsequent parameter lists* in a curried invocation, not to other parameters in the same list. When defining methods with parameters whose type constraints can only be satisfied if the type bindings for earlier parameters of the same method are known, use curried method definitions rather than single parameter lists.

Puzzler 7

Caught Up in Closures

Function values, especially anonymous functions, provide a convenient and concise way to create and pass around "portable" snippets of code. This is enhanced by allowing these snippets to reference values in scope when the function is defined, beyond just the immediate function parameters.

The following code creates "delayed accessors" for a set of values and invokes them later. What is the result of executing this code in the REPL?

```scala
import collection.mutable.Buffer

val accessors1 = Buffer.empty[() => Int]
val accessors2 = Buffer.empty[() => Int]

val data = Seq(100, 110, 120)
var j = 0
for (i <- 0 until data.length) {
  accessors1 += (() => data(i))
  accessors2 += (() => data(j))
  j += 1
}

accessors1.foreach(a1 => println(a1()))
accessors2.foreach(a2 => println(a2()))
```

Possibilities

1. The first statement prints:

37

```
100
110
120
```

and the second throws an IndexOutOfBoundsException.

2. Both statements print:

```
100
110
120
```

3. Both statements fail to compile with the error message: "not found: value data."

4. Both statements print:

```
120
120
120
```

Explanation

Since data, i, and j are no longer in scope when the functions are invoked, you may wonder whether the code compiles at all. Or you may wonder whether the functions all see the *last* value of data(i) and data(j), and, as a result, both print:

```
120
120
120
```

As it happens, the code does compile, and the first statement prints the expected values 100, 110, 120. The second statement never gets going, immediately throwing a runtime exception:

```
scala> accessors1.foreach(a1 => println(a1()))
100
110
120

scala> accessors2.foreach(a2 => println(a2()))
java.lang.IndexOutOfBoundsException: 3
  at scala.collection.LinearSeqOptimized$class.apply(
    LinearSeqOptimized.scala:51)
  at scala.collection.immutable.List.apply(List.scala:85)
  at $anonfun$1$$anonfun$apply$mcVI$sp$2.apply$mcI$sp(
    <console>:16)
  at $anonfun$1.apply(<console>:10)
  ...
```

The correct answer, therefore, is number 1.

Before examining which differences between i and j result in the observed behavior, it is helpful to look at how Scala enables the function body to access these variables at all.

Scala allows the body of a function to reference variables that are not explicit function parameters, but are in scope at the moment the function is constructed. To access these *free variables* when the function is invoked in a different scope, Scala "closes over" them to create a *closure*.

Closing over a free variable is not taking a "snapshot" of the variable's value when it is used. Instead, a field referencing the captured variable is added to the function object. Crucially for this case, while captured vals are simply represented by the value, capturing a var results in a *reference* to the var itself.

As an illustration, consider the following fun method:

```
def fun: () => Int = {
  val i = 1
  var j = 2
  () => i + j
}
```

The function returned from the fun method is a closure that captures one val, i, and one var, j. You can examine how the compiler treats i and j differently by invoking scala with the -print option, which prints the code with all Scala-specific features removed:

```scala
def fun(): Function0 = {
  val i: Int = 1;
  var j: runtime.IntRef = new runtime.IntRef(2);
  {
    (new anonymous class anonfunfun1(Illustration.this,
        i, j): Function0)
  }
};
```

Do you see the difference? The val is stored as a regular Int; the var instead becomes a scala.runtime.IntRef, a reference to a mutable (Java) int.

From here, the explanation for the observed behavior is straightforward: when each accessors1 function is created, it captures the current value of i, and so prints the expected results when invoked. The accessors2 functions, on the other hand, each capture a reference to a mutable IntRef object containing the value of j, which can change over time.

By the time the first accessors2 function is invoked, the value of j is already 3. Since data only has three elements, invoking data(j) triggers an IndexOutOfBoundsException.

Discussion

The most robust way to prevent this problem is to avoid vars, which is also better Scala style. If you can't avoid a var, but you still want a closure to capture its value at the time the closure is created, you can "freeze" the var by assigning its value to a temporary val. Here's an example:

```scala
import collection.mutable.Buffer

val accessors2 = Buffer.empty[() => Int]

val data = Seq(100, 110, 120)
var j = 0
for (i <- 0 until data.length) {
  val currentJ = j
  accessors2 += (() => data(currentJ))
  j += 1
}
```

```
scala> accessors2.foreach(a2 => println(a2()))
100
110
120
```

 Avoid capturing free variables in your closures that refer to anything mutable—vars or mutable objects. If you need to close over anything mutable, extract a stable value and assign it to a val, then use that val in your function.

Puzzler 8

Map Comprehension

Scala's `for` comprehensions provide an elegant syntax for invocations of powerful functional constructs based on `map` and `flatMap`. In Scala, `for` comprehensions are so widespread that understanding how they are desugared to `map`, `flatMap`, `withFilter`, and `foreach` calls is a common exercise when learning the language. This is especially useful because it may sometimes be preferable to desugar a `for` comprehension "by hand," if only for debugging purposes.

In this puzzler, we compare a `for` comprehension that also uses a pattern match with a desugared version of the same `for` expression obtained by transforming:

```
for (i <- expr) yield fun(i)
```

to:

```
expr map { i => fun(i) }
```

What is the result of executing the following code in the REPL?

```
val xs = Seq(Seq("a", "b", "c"), Seq("d", "e", "f"),
             Seq("g", "h"), Seq("i", "j", "k"))
val ys = for (Seq(x, y, z) <- xs) yield x + y + z
val zs = xs map { case Seq(x, y, z) => x + y + z }
```

Possibilities

1. Evaluating both ys and zs throws a `MatchError`.

2. Both ys and zs evaluate to:

   ```
   Seq(abc, def, ijk)
   ```

3. Evaluating ys throws a `MatchError`, and zs evaluates to:

   ```
   Seq(abc, def, ijk)
   ```

4. ys evaluates to:

   ```
   Seq(abc, def, ijk)
   ```

   and evaluating zs throws a `MatchError`.

Explanation

Looking at the code sample in detail, you may note that Seq("g", "h") in xs doesn't actually match the Seq(x, y, z) pattern used in the for comprehension and the desugared map. So if you suspect that ys and zs don't transparently skip this value, you would assume that both would throw a MatchError. But surely the for comprehension and the desugared map call will behave in the same way?

That assumption would be wrong. The correct answer is number 4:

```
scala> val ys = for (Seq(x, y, z) <- xs) yield x + y + z
ys: Seq[String] = List(abc, def, ijk)

scala> val zs = xs map { case Seq(x, y, z) => x + y + z }
scala.MatchError: List(g, h) (of class
    scala.collection.immutable.$colon$colon)
  at $anonfun$1.apply(<console>:8)
  at $anonfun$1.apply(<console>:8)
  at scala.collection.TraversableLike$$anonfun$map$1.
    apply(TraversableLike.scala:245)
  ...
```

While the for comprehension skips the problematic value, the direct map invocation fails. To explain what is going on here, start by looking at this very simple for comprehension:

```
for (i <- 0 to 1) yield i + 1
```

This is desugared using the same scheme applied in the example:

```
0 to 1 map { i => i + 1 }
```

You can observe this desugaring in the REPL by starting the session with the -Xprint:parser setting:[1]

```
scala> for (i <- 0 to 1) yield i + 1
[[syntax trees at end of          parser]] // <console>
    ...
    val res2 = 0.to(1).map(((i) => i.$plus(1)))
```

In Scala, the i <- 0 to 1 syntax is called a *generator*. With generators that perform a simple variable assignment, it's easy to forget that the generator's left-hand side is not a simple variable, it's a *pattern*, as demonstrated by Seq(x, y, z) <- xs in the code sample. The Scala compiler desugars generators with non-trivial patterns (*i.e.*, patterns that constistute more than a simple variable assignment) differently. This expression:

```
for (pattern <- expr) yield fun
```

ends up being rewritten as:

```
expr map { case pattern => fun }
```

For example:

```
scala> for (i@j <- 0 to 1) yield i + j
[[syntax trees at end of          parser]] // <console>
    ...
    val res0 = 0.to(1).map(((x$1) => x$1:
        @scala.unchecked match {
      case (i @ (j @ _)) => i.$plus(j)
    }))
```

---

[1] The compiler argument -Xprint:<phase> prints the program code after specific compiler phases. scala -Xshow-phases displays a list of the phases, the first of which is parser.

So far, this is identical to our own desugaring in the example. But what the language specification *also* stipulates for a non-trivial pattern is the addition of a withFilter invocation.[2] Thus the following expression:

```
for (pattern <- expr) yield fun
```

actually becomes:

```
expr withFilter {
  case pattern => true
  case _ => false
} map { case pattern => fun }
```

It is this withFilter invocation that transparently "strips out" the non-matching value that causes the MatchError in our attempted desugaring.

Discussion

You can treat pattern matching generators in for comprehensions as including an "if matches" guard—guards are desugared to withFilter invocations. Adding this into the desugared version produces the expected result:

```
scala> xs withFilter { case Seq(x, y, z) => true; case _ =>
         false } map { case Seq(x, y, z) => x + y + z }
res1: Seq[String] = List(abc, def, ijk)
```

Because for comprehensions are very common in Scala code, familiarizing yourself with how for expressions are desugared is time well spent.

---

[2]Unlike filter, which creates a *new* collection and so incurs the overhead of an entire run through the source collection, withFilter is simply a "view." It lazily restricts the items passed on to subsequent map, flatMap, foreach, and withFilter calls and is specifically designed for efficient chaining of these operations.

Puzzler 9

Init You, Init Me

As your programs get larger, you may end up with modules that have cyclic dependencies. Reliably initializing such modules can be challenging.

What is the result of executing the following code in the REPL?

```
object XY {
  object X {
    val value: Int = Y.value + 1
  }
  object Y {
    val value: Int = X.value + 1
  }
}
println(if (math.random > 0.5) XY.X.value else XY.Y.value)
```

Possibilities

1. Prints:

   1

2. Prints:

   2

3. Prints either:

    1

    or:

    2

4. Throws a runtime exception.

Explanation

You may wonder whether the Scala compiler can even handle cyclic definitions of this kind, or whether you will run into an endless loop at runtime.

If you are confident that Scala can indeed handle such definitions without blowing up, you may suspect that the values will be initialized in declaration order. Since you randomly print either the value that is declared first (XY.X.value) or second (XY.Y.value), you would expect to see a non-deterministic result in this case.

Alternatively, you may guess that, while initializing the object *accessed* first, you will see default values for the other as-yet-uninitialized object, resulting in 1 being printed every time.

In fact, the correct answer is number 2. The value 2 is printed every time:

```
scala> println(if (math.random > 0.5) XY.X.value else
         XY.Y.value)
2

scala> println(s"X: ${XY.X.value} Y: ${XY.Y.value}")
X: 2 Y: 1
```

And after a few :reset commands, you should eventually see:[1]

```
scala> println(if (math.random > 0.5) XY.X.value else
         XY.Y.value)
2
```

---

[1]The :reset command tells the REPL to "forget" all definitions, allowing you to initialize XY.X.value and XY.Y.value again.

```
scala> println(s"X: ${XY.X.value} Y: ${XY.Y.value}")
X: 1 Y: 2
```

To understand what is going on, we'll first demonstrate that the Scala compiler has no problem with cycles in val definitions. It does, however, require at least one explicit type specification:

```
scala> lazy val x = y; lazy val y = x
<console>:12: error: recursive value y needs type
        lazy val x = y; lazy val y = x
                 ^

scala> lazy val x: Int = y; lazy val y = x
x: Int = <lazy>
y: Int = <lazy>
```

The language specification says that "the value defined by an object definition is instantiated lazily,"[2] and goes even further by remarking that an object can indeed be seen as "roughly equivalent to [...] a lazy value." This explains why the random choice of printing XY.X.value or XY.Y.value does not influence the outcome: the declaration order is irrelevant, since the values are not initialized when the objects are *declared*, but when they are *accessed*. The chosen object is always the first to be initialized, and the object initialized first ends up with the value 2.

But how does the object initialized first end up with the value 2, and why do you not run into an endless loop once you access it? Here, it helps to examine the output produced by the compiler when you compile just the XY object with scalac -print:

```
[[syntax trees at end of          cleanup]] // XY.scala
package <empty> {
  object XY extends Object {
    def <init>(): XY.type = {
      XY.super.<init>();
      ()
    }
  };
  object XY$X extends Object {
```

---

[2]Odersky, *The Scala Language Specification*, Section 5.4. [Ode14]

```
  private[this] val value: Int = _;
  <stable> <accessor> def value(): Int = XY$X.this.value;
  def <init>(): XY$X.type = {
    XY$X.super.<init>();
    XY$X.this.value = XY$Y.value().+(1);
    ()
  }
};
object XY$Y extends Object {
  private[this] val value: Int = _;
  <stable> <accessor> def value(): Int = XY$Y.this.value;
  def <init>(): XY$Y.type = {
    XY$Y.super.<init>();
    XY$Y.this.value = XY$X.value().+(1);
    ()
  }
}
}
```

What happens when you access the randomly chosen object? Assume you are trying to get XY.Y.value:

1. XY is initialized by calling its constructor. Uneventful.

2. XY$Y is, in turn, initialized by calling *its* constructor, which attempts to get X's value through the accessor, XY$X.value().

3. The call to XY$X.value() triggers the initialization of XY$X, again, through its constructor. Therefore, it now tries to retrieve the value for Y by calling XY$Y.value().

4. At this point, Y has still not been initialized, so you seem to be on the brink of an endless loop. But now "magic" happens: the JVM specification stipulates that instances cannot be initialized multiple times.[3] As a result, XY$X *directly invokes* XY$Y's accessor method value(), which, since the value has not yet been defined, returns 0, the default value for the Int type.

---

[3]Lindholm, *et al.*, *The Java Virtual Machine Specification*, Section 5.5. [Lin13]

5. Given this value 0, the constructor of XY$X can now complete the initialization of XY$X.this.value, setting it to 1 and returning.

6. At last, the call to XY$X.value() in XY$Y's constructor can proceed, returning the value 1.

7. Given this value 1, the constructor of XY$Y completes the assignment of XY$Y.this.value, setting it to 2.

If you happen to choose XY.X.value as the value to print, the initialization takes place with roles reversed. This explains why the first-accessed object will always receive a value of 2, with 1 being assigned to the value of the other object.

Discussion

The observed behavior becomes more surprising when you compare it to what happens with similar kinds of cyclic definitions. For example, given that *The Scala Language Specification* says that objects are "roughly equivalent to [lazy values]," you might try:[4]

```
object XY2 {
  lazy val xvalue: Int = yvalue + 1
  lazy val yvalue: Int = xvalue + 1
}
scala> println(if (math.random > 0.5) XY2.xvalue else
         XY2.yvalue)
java.lang.StackOverflowError
  ...
  at XY2$.xvalue(<console>:8)
  at XY2$.yvalue$lzycompute(<console>:9)
  at XY2$.yvalue(<console>:9)
  at XY2$.xvalue$lzycompute(<console>:8)
  at XY2$.xvalue(<console>:8)
```

Or you could stick with objects, but put them inside an enclosing class instead of an object:

---

[4]See Puzzler 4 for a more detailed discussion of initialization options for variables.

```scala
class XY3 {
  object X {
    val value: Int = Y.value + 1
  }
  object Y {
    val value: Int = X.value + 1
  }
}
scala> val xy3 = new XY3()
xy3: XY3 = XY3@770b07b9

scala> println(if (math.random > 0.5) xy3.X.value else
         xy3.Y.value)
java.lang.StackOverflowError
  ...
  at XY3.Y$lzycompute(<console>:11)
  at XY3.Y(<console>:11)
  at XY3$X$.<init>(<console>:9)
  at XY3.X$lzycompute(<console>:8)
  at XY3.X(<console>:8)
  at XY3$Y$.<init>(<console>:12)
  at XY3.Y$lzycompute(<console>:11)
```

In both cases, you are missing the "endless loop protection" provided by the JVM's inability to initialize the *same* instance more than once. The compiler happily allows two functions to each each other, so you throw an exception at runtime.

In the second example, `Y$lzycompute` starts creating a new instance of Y to assign to the XY.Y singleton. This tries to access XY.X, which triggers X$lzycompute and, because XY.Y has not been initialized yet, invokes Y$lzycompute again. Y$lzycompute tries to create *another* instance of Y, and so on.

Alternatively, you can be slightly "less lazy":

```scala
object XY4 {
  lazy val xvalue: Int = yvalue + 1
  val yvalue: Int = xvalue + 1
}
```

52

```scala
scala> println(if (math.random > 0.5) XY4.xvalue else
      XY4.yvalue)
2

scala> println(s"X: ${XY4.xvalue} Y: ${XY4.yvalue}")
X: 1 Y: 2
```

Now, it is no longer the order in which the values are accessed that determines their values: for XY4, yvalue will be evaluated as soon as XY4 is initialized. This triggers the evaluation of xvalue, which sees the default value 0 for yvalue and becomes 1, with yvalue always becoming 2. The order in which xvalue and yvalue are declared still does not matter, though:

```scala
object XY4a {
  val yvalue: Int = xvalue + 1
  lazy val xvalue: Int = yvalue + 1
}
```

```scala
scala> println(if (math.random > 0.5) XY4a.xvalue else
      XY4a.yvalue)
1

scala> println(s"X: ${XY4a.xvalue} Y: ${XY4a.yvalue}")
X: 1 Y: 2
```

You can also avoid lazy values entirely:

```scala
object XY5 {
  val xvalue: Int = yvalue + 1
  val yvalue: Int = xvalue + 1
}
```

```scala
scala> println(if (math.random > 0.5) XY5.xvalue else
      XY5.yvalue)
1

scala> println(s"X: ${XY5.xvalue} Y: ${XY5.yvalue}")
X: 1 Y: 2
```

Here, *both* xvalue and yvalue are immediately evaluated on initialization of XY5. xvalue tries to retrieve the value of the as-yet-unassigned yvalue, again sees the default value 0, and is set to 1. yvalue is then always set to 2. Here, though, the problem is so predictable that the compiler emits a warning as soon as XY5 is defined:

```
scala> object XY5 {
           val xvalue: Int = yvalue + 1
           val yvalue: Int = xvalue + 1
       }
<console>:8: warning: Reference to uninitialized value yvalue
           val xvalue: Int = yvalue + 1
                               ^

defined object XY5
```

Furthermore, unlike the other examples, here the *declaration* order determines the values of xvalue and yvalue. Inverting the order flips the values:

```
object XY5a {
  val yvalue: Int = xvalue + 1
  val xvalue: Int = yvalue + 1
}
scala> println(s"X: ${XY5a.xvalue} Y: ${XY5a.yvalue}")
X: 2 Y: 1
```

In summary, cyclic dependencies and definitions are tricky and hard to reason about. Some forms are dependent on the declaration order, others on the order of initialization, yet others result in endless loops. Avoid them where possible.

 Avoid cyclic dependencies and definitions where possible. If you really can find no way to remove the cycle, ensure you understand the initialization behavior of all its components and values. Test thoroughly to ensure you get the intended result, especially if the order in which elements will be initialized is not deterministic.

Puzzler 10

A Case of Equality

Scala's case classes are an easy way to represent entities, with factory methods, extractors, and several convenience methods implemented "for free":

```
class Country(val isoCode: String, val name: String)
case class CountryCC(isoCode: String, name: String)

val homeOfScala = new Country("CH", "Switzerland")
val homeOfScalaCC =
  CountryCC("CH", "Switzerland") // factory method

scala> println(homeOfScala equals
        new Country("CH", "Switzerland"))
false

scala> println(homeOfScalaCC equals
        CountryCC("CH", "Switzerland"))
true

scala> println(homeOfScala.toString)
$line348.$read$$iw$$iw$Country@39eb8ede

scala> println(homeOfScalaCC.toString)
CountryCC(CH,Switzerland)
```

To give you a better idea of what's going on, we'll trace the invocation of hashCode, one of the convenience methods. We'll mix a "debugging" trait into the declaration or instantiations of the case class, then add case class instances to HashSets to see how hashCode is used. What is the result of executing the following code in the REPL?

```
trait TraceHashCode {
  override def hashCode: Int = {
    println(s"TRACE: In hashCode for ${this}")
    super.hashCode
  }
}


// mix in trait at instantiation
case class Country(isoCode: String)
def newSwitzInst = new Country("CH") with TraceHashCode


// mix in trait at declaration time
case class CountryWithTrace(isoCode: String) extends
  TraceHashCode
def newSwitzDecl = CountryWithTrace("CH")


import collection.immutable.HashSet
val countriesInst = HashSet(newSwitzInst)
println(countriesInst.iterator contains newSwitzInst)
println(countriesInst contains newSwitzInst)


val countriesDecl = HashSet(newSwitzDecl)
println(countriesDecl.iterator contains newSwitzDecl)
println(countriesDecl contains newSwitzDecl)
```

Possibilities

1. Prints:

```
true
TRACE: In hashCode for Country(CH)
true
true
TRACE: In hashCode for CountryWithTrace(CH)
true
```

2. Prints:

```
true
TRACE: In hashCode for Country(CH)
true
true
TRACE: In hashCode for CountryWithTrace(CH)
false
```

3. Prints:

```
true
TRACE: In hashCode for Country(CH)
false
true
TRACE: In hashCode for CountryWithTrace(CH)
false
```

4. Prints:

```
true
TRACE: In hashCode for Country(CH)
true
false
TRACE: In hashCode for CountryWithTrace(CH)
false
```

Explanation

The generated implementation of equals and hashCode for case classes is based on *structural equality*: two instances are equal if they have the same type and equal constructor arguments. Since mixing in TraceHashCode does not affect that structure, you might assume that instances created by newSwitzInst are equal and have identical hash codes, and the same holds true for newSwitzDecl. And if this is true, countriesInst should contain newSwitzInst, and countriesDecl should contain newSwitzDecl.

Or, you may wonder whether mixing in `TraceHashCode` at declaration time "switches off" the generated structural equality for `CountryWithTrace`. Different instances created by `newSwitzDecl` would have different hash codes and not be considered equal, and therefore the second instance created by `newSwitzDecl` would *not* be a member of `countriesDecl`. Surely, though, it makes no difference whether you check the set or the iterator?

Actually, it does. Mixing in `TraceHashCode` on instantiation leaves `equals` and `hashCode` behavior unaffected, as you might hope. But declaring `CountryWithTrace` as extending from `TraceHashCode` switches off the generated `hashCode` method for case classes, so the new instance created by `newSwitzDecl` is not found in the set. The generated `equals` implementation, on which the iterator depends, is *not* affected. The correct answer is number 2:

```scala
scala> println(countriesInst.iterator contains
         newSwitzInst)
true

scala> println(countriesInst contains newSwitzInst)
TRACE: In hashCode for Country(CH)
true

scala> println(countriesDecl.iterator contains
         newSwitzDecl)
true

scala> println(countriesDecl contains newSwitzDecl)
TRACE: In hashCode for CountryWithTrace(CH)
false
```

This is especially problematic because you are inadvertently violating the equals/hashCode contract here, which states, "it is required that if two objects are equal [...] they have identical hash codes."[1] Note that both instances created by `newSwitzInst` *are* considered equal (and have equal hash codes), so mixing in `TraceHashCode` at *instantiation time* does not have any unintended effects.

The language specification's explanation of case classes[2] can help clarify what is going on (our emphasis):

---

[1] See the Scaladoc for `scala.Any`. [EPF]

[2] Odersky, *The Scala Language Specification*, Section 5.3.2. [Ode14]

Every case class implicitly overrides some method definitions of class scala.AnyRef *unless* a definition of the same method is already given in the case class itself or *a concrete definition of the same method is given in some base class of the case class* different from AnyRef.

So the compiler will generate overrides only if explicit implementations of the methods are not present in the case class or inherited from a parent class or trait. In addition, the conditions under which the methods (equals and hashCode, in this case) are overridden are *independent of each other*, so coherence between equals and hashCode is left to the developer.

In our example, the compiler generates an overridden implementation for CountryWithTrace's equals method, so comparing two instances created by newSwitzDecl via newSwitzDecl == newSwitzDecl evaluates to true. The hashCode method, however, is *not* overridden, so the super.hashCode call in TraceHashCode invokes the default implementation in AnyRef, which is consistent with reference equality. Hence, newSwitzDecl.hashCode == newSwitzDecl.hashCode returns false, and therefore new instances created by newSwitzDecl are not found in the countriesDecl set.

In the case of new Country("CH") with TraceHashCode, the generated overrides are added by the compiler when case class Country is declared, at which point neither equals nor hashCode are explicitly implemented. By the time TraceHashCode is mixed in during the creation of new instances by newSwitzInst, Country already has an equals method based on structural equality. The super.hashCode call in TraceHashCode thus invokes the compiler-generated hashCode method in Country, as intended.

Discussion

Adding the "debugging" trait at *instantiation* time seems to be the way to go. However, you want to avoid having to mix in the TraceHashCode trait every time you create an instance. You can achieve this by (temporarily) creating a subclass of Country:

```scala
case class _Country(isoCode: String) // renamed
// use :paste in the REPL
class Country(isoCode: String) extends
  _Country(isoCode: String) with TraceHashCode
```

```
object Country {
  def apply(isoCode: String): Country = new Country(isoCode)
}
// ctrl-D to end :paste mode
def newSwitzSubcl = Country("CH")

scala> println(newSwitzSubcl == newSwitzSubcl)
true

scala> println(newSwitzSubcl.hashCode
         == newSwitzSubcl.hashCode)
TRACE: In hashCode for _Country(CH)
TRACE: In hashCode for _Country(CH)
true
```

Extending case classes is not considered good practice, however. You can do a little better by "replacing" the case class factory method. The compiler will still attempt to generate an `apply` method if you define one yourself, however, which will cause a compiler error. If you want to redefine the standard `apply` factory method in a case class's companion object, you will need to declare the case class `abstract`:

```
// use :paste in the REPL
abstract case class Country(isoCode: String)
object Country {
  def apply(isoCode: String): Country =
    new Country(isoCode) with TraceHashCode
}
// ctrl-D to end :paste mode
def newSwitzFact = Country("CH")

scala> println(newSwitzFact == newSwitzFact)
true

scala> println(newSwitzFact.hashCode
         == newSwitzFact.hashCode)
TRACE: In hashCode for Country(CH)
TRACE: In hashCode for Country(CH)
true
```

Conveniently, the compiler will still add an implementation of `unapply` to the companion object, so your case class will still work with pattern matching. You will, however, be unable to make instances using new—*i.e.*, new Country("CH")—since Country is now abstract.

If you are going to mess with the declaration of the case class, the easiest approach is to avoid super.hashCode and simply ensure that the implementation of hashCode is consistent with structural equality. Calling isoCode.hashCode would meet this requirement, but you have to be careful since isoCode could conceivably be null. The ## method, Scala's null-safe version of hashCode, avoids this problem:

```
case class CountryWithTrace(isoCode: String) {
  // avoiding super.hashCode
  override def hashCode: Int = {
    println(s"TRACE: In hashCode for ${this}")
    isoCode.##
  }
}
def newSwitzHCImpl = CountryWithTrace("CH")

scala> println(newSwitzHCImpl == newSwitzHCImpl)
true

scala> println(newSwitzHCImpl.hashCode
         == newSwitzHCImpl.hashCode)
TRACE: In hashCode for CountryWithTrace(CH)
TRACE: In hashCode for CountryWithTrace(CH)
true
```

 When supplying your own implementation of equals or hashCode for a case class:

1. Ensure that it obeys structural equality if specifying only one of the two methods.

2. If not, implement *both* methods according to the equals/hashCode contract.

Puzzler 11

If at First You Don't Succeed...

By default, Scala performs strict evaluation: expressions are evaluated eagerly, as soon as they are defined. However, as discussed in detail in Puzzler 4, Scala also supports lazy (non-strict) evaluation, where variables are not initialized until they are referenced for the first time.

Evaluation of expressions, strict or non-strict, may result in an exception, which can cause some interesting behavior. The following program illustrates such a situation. What does it do?

```scala
var x = 0
lazy val y = 1 / x

try {
  println(y)
} catch {
  case _: Exception =>
    x = 1
    println(y)
}
```

Possibilities

1. Throws an ArithmeticException: / by zero.

2. Prints:

   1

63

3. Prints:

```
Infinity
```

4. Prints:

```
<lazy>
```

Explanation

First we'll walk through the program and consider some possible outcomes. Value y is declared as lazy, so its initialization is deferred until it is accessed for the first time, which happens to be in the first call to `println`. At that point, a runtime exception could be thrown (division by zero), with y remaining undefined and marked as `lazy`:

```
scala> var x = 0
x: Int = 0

scala> lazy val y = 1 / x
y: Int = <lazy>
```

In the `catch` block, the second call to `println` would output the current, still uninitialized, state of y: `<lazy>`. Reassigning 1 to variable x would have no observable effect.

Or, if y is still uninitialized when the `try` block is entered, the second call to `println` in the `catch` block might try to initialize the variable once again. This would result in the original "divide by zero" exception being thrown anew.

Alternatively, it is conceivable that dividing 1 by 0 evaluates to `Infinity` (the third candidate answer), which is what it represents mathematically. You can see what actually happens if you run the code in the REPL:

```
scala> try {
         println(y)
       } catch {
         case _: Exception =>
           x = 1
```

```
    println(y)
  }
1
x: Int = 1
y: Int = <lazy>
```

Quite a surprise, right? The correct answer is number 2! Given that the code prints 1, perhaps the x = 1 statement makes a difference? As a matter of fact, it does. In addition to a postponed evaluation, lazy values have the interesting property that if an exception is thrown during their initialization, they will be recomputed when accessed again.[1] This is exactly what happens during the second call to println, and that is why it outputs 1.

Discussion

The expression 1 / x is certainly not so expensive as to make y benefit from being a lazy val. Here's how you might define y as a strict val:

```
var x = 0
val y = try {
  1 / x
} catch {
  case _: Exception =>
    x = 1
    1 / x
}
println(y)
```

This code produces the expected result, but here you only get the one additional chance to initialize y properly—in the catch block. Every time uninitialized lazy vals are accessed, on the other hand, they will go through their initialization phase until they are successfully initialized.

This characteristic of lazy vals means they can be useful in situations where initialization depends on a resource that might not be immediately available. For instance, suppose that during server startup a certain file will be generated from data that takes some time to fetch.

---

[1]Odersky, *The Scala Language Specification*, Section 5.2. [Ode14]

For example, say you want to introduce a public variable that depends on the content of the eventually generated file, and that you do not want to block a thread waiting for the file contents to be written. One elegant approach to solving this would be to define the variable as a `lazy val` that simply assumes the file is available:

```scala
import io.Source
lazy val res = Source.fromFile("./processing-result.txt").
  getLines.filter(_.contains("quux"))
```

If `res` is referenced before the file is available, it will throw an exception during initialization and signal to the calling code that the collection of data has not been completed. Once the result file is written, `res` will be properly initialized and will then hold the expected value.

 Scala will reattempt to initialize `lazy val`s on each access until initialization succeeds. This makes them a useful option for postponed resource initialization.

Puzzler 12

To Map, or Not to Map

Alongside standard functional idioms, such as `for` comprehensions and the combinators `map` and `flatMap`, Scala supports imperative operations on collections through `for` loops and the `foreach` method.

In this puzzler, both kinds of operations–functional and imperative–are used used to print the Roman numeral symbols in ascending order. What is the result of executing the following code in the REPL?

```scala
case class RomanNumeral(symbol: String, value: Int)

implicit object RomanOrdering extends Ordering[RomanNumeral] {
  def compare(a: RomanNumeral, b: RomanNumeral) =
    a.value compare b.value
}

import collection.immutable.SortedSet

val numerals = SortedSet(
  RomanNumeral("M", 1000),
  RomanNumeral("C", 100),
  RomanNumeral("X", 10),
  RomanNumeral("I", 1),
  RomanNumeral("D", 500),
  RomanNumeral("L", 50),
  RomanNumeral("V", 5)
)

println("Roman numeral symbols for 1 5 10 50 100 500 1000:")
for (num <- numerals; sym = num.symbol) { print(s"${sym} ") }
numerals map { _.symbol } foreach { sym => print(s"${sym} ") }
```

Possibilities

1. Prints:

```
Roman numeral symbols for 1 5 10 50 100 500 1000:
I V X L C D M
C D I L M V X
```

2. Prints:

```
Roman numeral symbols for 1 5 10 50 100 500 1000:
M C X I D L V
M C X I D L V
```

3. Prints:

```
Roman numeral symbols for 1 5 10 50 100 500 1000:
I V X L C D M
I V X L C D M
```

4. Prints:

```
Roman numeral symbols for 1 5 10 50 100 500 1000:
C D I L M V X
I V X L C D M
```

Explanation

On the basis of the candidate answers, what you have to determine is which iteration order is applicable to the invocations: the order in which the numerals were *added to the set*, the order of their *values*, or of their *symbols*.

Since you are dealing with a sorted set you may assume that the sort order, rather than the declaration order, will determine the iteration sequence. And the ordering appears to be correctly implemented, based on the value. So surely both statements should iterate through the numerals in ascending numerical value and print I V X L C D M?

Not so—the correct answer is number 1:

```
Roman numeral symbols for 1 5 10 50 100 500 1000:
scala> for (num <- numerals; sym = num.symbol) {
         print(s"${sym} ") }
I V X L C D M
scala> numerals map { _.symbol } foreach { sym =>
         print(s"${sym} ") }
C D I L M V X
```

To start to understand the result, examine the first statement, which behaves as expected. According to *The Scala Language Specification*, a simple for (i <- expr) { fun(i) } loop is desugared to an invocation of the foreach method: expr foreach { i => fun(i) }.[1]

In this case, the for loop is not quite so simple, because of the additional *value definition*,[2] sym = num.symbol. To be able to pass both num and sym into the loop body, the compiler replaces numerals in the generator by a collection of (num, sym) tuples. It then invokes foreach on this collection of *tuples* and extracts both elements from the tuple before passing them to the actual loop body.[3] In short, the for loop is desugared roughly to the following:

```
numerals map { num =>
  val sym = num.symbol
  (num, sym)
} foreach { case (num, sym) =>
  println(sym)
}
```

This turns out to be surprisingly similar to the second statement:

```
numerals map { num => num.symbol } foreach { ... }
```

In *both* cases, therefore, foreach is not invoked on the original numerals set, but on the result of the map invocation. This, in turn, explains the different results.

---

[1] Odersky, *The Scala Language Specification*, Section 6.19. [Ode14]
[2] Ibid.
[3] Ibid.

69

What does map return? One of the main features of Scala collections is that transformations, such as map, *preserve the type of the collection*. In this case, the result is thus not an arbitrary collection with the same iteration order as the original, but a new SortedSet. This new SortedSet's iteration order is determined by *its* elements, not by the order of the elements in the original collection.

Since tuples are ordered first by their first elements,[4] which are simply the elements of numerals in succession, the iteration order of numerals and the sorted set of tuples is the same. As a result, the symbols are printed in the expected sequence, *i.e.*, in order of ascending value.

The set of symbols that is created in the second statement, however, is a sorted set of *strings*, and is consequently ordered lexicographically. For this reason, the second statement prints the symbols alphabetically, rather than in the expected order of increasing value.

Discussion

Of course, in this particular case you can simply avoid the intermediate map and iterate over numerals directly, avoiding the unexpected reordering *and* an unnecessary iteration over the collection:

```scala
scala> for (num <- numerals) { print(s"${num.symbol} ") }
I V X L C D M
scala> numerals foreach { num => print(s"${num.symbol} ") }
I V X L C D M
```

In the general case, a possible alternative is to apply the transformation to a *view*[5] of the original collection:

```scala
scala> numerals.view map { _.symbol } foreach { sym =>
         print(s"${sym} ") }
I V X L C D M
```

Calling map on the view does *not* create an intermediate SortedSet. Instead, the num => num.symbol operation is applied lazily, only when the next ele-

---

[4]See the Scaladoc for scala.math.Ordering. [EPF]

[5]See section "Views" in the Scala collections library documentation. [Odea]

ment of the transformed `numerals` collection is retrieved and printed in the
`foreach` loop.

The iteration order of the view is identical to that of the original collection, so the symbols are printed in the intended sequence.

As of Scala 2.11, however, there is still significant debate regarding the usability of views. A simple alternative is to start with a collection type whose iteration order is not affected by transformations, such as Seq:

```
scala> numerals.toSeq map { _.symbol } foreach { sym =>
        print(s"${sym} ") }
 I V X L C D M
```

This usually comes at the cost of an additional iteration over the original collection, but it's easy and straightforward to use.

 If you are carrying out transformations on a collection, especially when chaining multiple operations, note that the iteration order of the original collection is not automatically preserved. Convert the original to a sequence if stable iteration order is required.

Puzzler 13

Self: See Self

Recursive variable definitions are a tricky problem in many languages. The simplest such definition is a variable that refers to itself.

The following code attempts to define two such variables. What is the result of executing it in the REPL?

```
val s1: String = s1
val s2: String = s2 + s2

println(s1.length)
println(s2.length)
```

Possibilities

1. Prints:

   0
   0

2. Both `println` statements throw a `NullPointerException`.

3. The first `println` statement throws a `NullPointerException`, and the second prints:

   8

4. Both `println` statements fail to compile.

Explanation

You may wonder whether self-references are allowed at all in Scala. Perhaps the compiler only complains if you apply an operation to the self-reference, as in the second statement.

Alternatively, you might assume that self-referential variables cause the default value to be assigned to the variable, which in this case would result in NullPointerExceptions.

As it happens, both statements indeed compile successfully. However, only one of them throws the anticipated runtime exception:

```
scala> println(s1.length)
java.lang.NullPointerException
   ...

scala> println(s2.length)
8
```

The correct answer, surprisingly enough, is number 3.

Before figuring out what is happening in the second example, it will help to examine how Scala treats recursive definitions of this kind generally. According to *The Scala Language Specification*, recursive value definitions are indeed valid in Scala.[1] The only condition is that the type of such values must be given explicitly:

```
scala> val s = s
<console>:7: error: recursive value s needs type
       val s = s
             ^
```

When the compiler evaluates the expression on the right-hand side of the assignment statement, it uses the default value for any uninitialized variables, as usual:

```
scala> val x = y; val y = 10
<console>:7: warning: Reference to uninitialized value y
       val x = y; val y = 10
             ^

x: Int = 0
y: Int = 10
```

---

[1] Odersky, *The Scala Language Specification*, Section 4.1. [Ode14]

The default value is also used for any occurrences of the variable itself, which is obviously also still uninitialized. In this case, therefore, s1 is assigned the value null, the default value for Strings and all AnyRefs:

```
scala> val s1: String = s1
<console>:7: warning: value s1 does nothing other than call
  itself recursively
        val s1: String = s1
                         ^

s1: String = null
```

What about s2? Here, similarly, all occurrences of s2 in its declaration are replaced by the default value null, so its initialization statement is null + null.

The Scala compiler converts the concatenation of two string constants into bytecode equivalent to:

```
String s2 = (new StringBuilder()).append(null)
              .append(null).toString();
```

This matches the behavior of Java, as described in the *Java Virtual Machine Specification*.[2] StringBuilder, in turn, converts the reference null into the string "null".[3] The value of s2 is thus the eight-character string, "nullnull":

```
scala> val s2: String = s2 + s2
s2: String = nullnull
```

Discussion

Self-referential definitions such as these are never required and should simply be avoided. The default value for the variable's type can be used in place of any self-reference. This is what the compiler will do in any case.

In many languages, such self-references are not even allowed. The Java compiler, for example, will complain:

---

[2]Lindholm, *et. al.*, *The Java Virtual Machine Specification*, Section 15.18.1.1. [Lin13]
[3]See the Javadoc for StringBuilder. [Ora]

```
public class SelfRef {
  String s = s + s;

  public static void main(String[] args) {
    System.out.println(new SelfRef().s.length());
  }
}
$ javac SelfRef.java
SelfRef.java:2: error: self-reference in initializer
  String s = s + s;
            ^

SelfRef.java:2: error: self-reference in initializer
  String s = s + s;
               ^

2 errors
```

Self-reference checking in Java is not very sophisticated, however, and is easily fooled:

```
public class SelfRef2 {
  String s = this.s + this.s; // fool the compiler

  public static void main(String[] args) {
    System.out.println(new SelfRef2().s.length());
  }
}
$ javac SelfRef2.java
$ java SelfRef2
8
```

 Avoid self-referential variable definitions: replace occurrences of the variable being defined with the default value for the variable's type.

Puzzler 14

Return to Me!

Unlike Java, Scala does not require methods returning a value to contain an explicit `return` statement. If omitted, the method will inherently return the result of the last expression.

Occasionally, though, explicit `return` statements do show up in Scala code. In fact, a single method can contain multiple *return expressions*, as in the following program. What does it do?

```
def sumItUp: Int = {
  def one(x: Int): Int = { return x; 1 }
  val two = (x: Int) => { return x; 2 }
  1 + one(2) + two(3)
}
println(sumItUp)
```

Possibilities

1. Prints:

   3

2. Prints:

   4

3. Prints:

   6

4. Fails to compile with an error: unreachable code.

Explanation

Something that immediately stands out in this code are the number literals, 1 and 2, which appear after `return` statements. Given their location in the code, they will never be reached. The compiler will likely detect this and fail with an unreachable code error. Therefore, candidate answer number 4 is the correct one, right?

Not so fast! *The Scala Language Specification* stipulates that anything following a return expression is not evaluated, *i.e.*, simply ignored.[1]

The unreachable literals 1 and 2 thus turn out to be a red herring. With those out of the way, surely some common sense can help identify the right answer. Both method one and function value two return the arguments passed to them, *i.e.*, 2 and 3, respectively. Therefore, the result is 6, so the third candidate answer must be the correct one.

This reasoning can easily be verified in the REPL:

```
scala> println(sumItUp)
3
```

Hmm... *not* the expected value 6. The correct answer is number 1! Let's go back to the code to see what we overlooked. The function literal defined for value two looks a bit odd because of the `return` statement. Was it a mistake to assume that the `return` keyword has the same semantics in a function body as in a method? Once again, the REPL is your friend:

```
scala> val two = (x: Int) => { return x; 2 }
<console>:7: error: return outside method definition
        val two = (x: Int) => { return x; 2 }
                                ^
```

---

[1] Odersky, *The Scala Language Specification*, Section 6.20. [Ode14]

78

Indeed, there is more to `return` than expected! Time to consult the language specification again:[2]

> A return expression `return e` must occur inside the body of some enclosing named method or function [`f`]. ... The return expression evaluates the expression e and returns its value as the result of f.

The enclosing *named method* for the first `return x` statement is method one. However, the enclosing named method for the second `return x` statement is not the function value `two`, but method `sumItUp`. And that is the essence of the puzzler. It might appear as if function value `two` should qualify as an enclosing named function, but only methods and local functions (`def`s) can act as the enclosing scope of `return` statements. So, when 3 is applied to function value `two`, it is immediately returned as a result of the entire method `sumItUp`. The result of the invocation of method one is ignored.

Discussion

Idiomatic Scala coding style does not encourage explicit return expressions and, in particular, methods with *multiple* `return` statements. This favors more concise, less complex methods.

Since use of explicit `return` statements is discouraged, you might be wondering if it is necessary to use them at all in a Scala program. After all, most of the time, explicit `return` statements can be replaced with equivalent expressions. As nearly all control structures in Scala are expressions, this is not difficult. For example, consider the following method:

```scala
def fibonacci(n: Int): Int = {
  if (n < 2) return n
  fibonacci(n - 1) + fibonacci(n - 2)
}
```

This method can be rewritten without `return` like this:

```scala
def fibonacci(n: Int): Int =
  if (n < 2) n
  else fibonacci(n - 1) + fibonacci(n - 2)
```

---

[2]Odersky, *The Scala Language Specification*, Section 6.20. [Ode14]

Your code can be rewritten in this way even if you want to return early from multiple places, when checking whether preconditions to your function are satisfied, for example. Those cases can be implemented as nested `if-else` expressions. By doing so, however, the normal path of execution can become less obvious.[3] In such situations, cutting the execution of a method short with a `return` can make the code more readable. Additionally, explicit `return` statements can be used for performance optimization, to escape out of a tight loop, for instance.

A return expression is required, however, to break out of multiple levels of nested functions. In such cases, the control flow has to jump out of *all* nested functions to the innermost enclosing method (*i.e.*, the first *method* around the `return`, as opposed to the innermost enclosing block).[4]

Suppose you wanted to implement a method that, for a given sequence of currencies, queries a web service to get the current exchange rate and returns the first currency whose rate change has exceeded a given threshold since the last query. Here is how that method might look:

```
def findHotCurrency[A](currencies: Seq[A],
    threshold: (Double, Double) => Boolean): Option[A] = {
  for (currency <- currencies) {
    val oldRate = getCurrentRate(currency)
    val newRate = fetchRate(currency)
    if (threshold(oldRate, newRate)) return Some(currency)
  }
  None
}
```

Note that the `return` statement in this example is in fact contained inside a nested function! Namely, since the Scala compiler translates a `for` expression:

```
for (x <- expr) body
```

into:

```
expr foreach (x => body)
```

---

[3]Fowler, *Refactoring: Improving the Design of Existing Code*. [Fow99]
[4]Griffith, "Purpose of `return` statement in Scala." [Gri10]

the body of the for becomes the body of a nested function that is passed to foreach. That also means that if you didn't explicitly return, as in:

```
if (threshold(oldRate, newRate)) Some(currency)
```

the code would still compile, but the method would incorrectly return None because the result of the function passed to foreach is always discarded.

The only other way to implement the same control flow is to throw and then catch an exception. As a matter of fact, returning from a nested anonymous function is implemented (by the compiler) by throwing and catching a scala.runtime.NonLocalReturnControl exception. This is why it is not a good idea to catch java.lang.Throwable in Scala: doing so might interfere with the control flow of return statements used in function literals.

Exception handling is, in general, an expensive operation. For that reason, return statements should be avoided in lambda functions in performance critical code, if possible.

Lastly, unreachable code (the fourth candidate answer) is actually a warning that's relevant only in the context of pattern matching, where a pattern can match everything and thus prevent subsequent cases from ever being reached.[5]

By default, the Scala compiler does not complain about other unreachable code. If desired, the -Ywarn-dead-code compiler option will warn you:

```
scala> def sumItUp: Int = {
         def one(x: Int): Int = { return x; 1 }
         val two = (x: Int) => { return x; 2 }
         1 + one(2) + two(3)
       }
<console>:8: warning: dead code following this construct
         def one(x: Int): Int = { return x; 1 }
                                  ^

<console>:9: warning: dead code following this construct
         val two = (x: Int) => { return x; 2 }
                                 ^

sumItUp: Int
```

---

[5] See Puzzler 2 for a more detailed discussion of pattern matching.

You can also take it one step further and use the –Xfatal-warnings flag, which will cause compilation to fail if there are any warnings.

 If possible, you should avoid using explicit return statements. If you need to use them, be conscious of the context and ensure the execution will resume where you intend. Be aware that return statements return only from methods and local functions, not from function values that may be defined within them.

Puzzler 15

Count Me Now, Count Me Later

Scala uses the underscore character (_) as a wildcard symbol quite extensively. The following program focuses on two uses of this symbol. What does it print?

```scala
var x = 0
def counter() = { x += 1; x }
def add(a: Int)(b: Int) = a + b
val adder1 = add(counter)(_)
val adder2 = add(counter) _

println("x = " + x)
println(adder1(10))
println("x = " + x)
println(adder2(10))
println("x = " + x)
```

Possibilities

1. Prints:

```
x = 1
12
x = 2
11
x = 2
```

83

2. Prints:

```
x = 1
11
x = 1
12
x = 2
```

3. Prints:

```
x = 0
11
x = 1
12
x = 2
```

4. Prints:

```
x = 2
11
x = 2
12
x = 2
```

Explanation

The lines that define `counter`, `adder1`, and `adder2` seem to be crucial in the code snippet, so let's focus on fully understanding them. The `counter` method definition contains an example of a side effect. When evaluated, the current value of x is incremented and returned, because in Scala, the last expression of a method is its return value.

The expressions defining `adder1` and `adder2` seem more interesting. They look deceptively similar and produce the same function value type:

```
scala> val adder1 = add(counter)(_)
adder1: Int => Int = <function1>
```

```
scala> val adder2 = add(counter) _
adder2: Int => Int = <function1>
```

Yet, their semantics are completely different. In the case of `adder1`, it might appear as if a function value is being created by partially applying method `add`. Actually, the underscore in this case is an example of placeholder syntax for anonymous functions.[1] For instance, consider the expression:

```
_ + 1
```

This is equivalent to an anonymous function:

```
x => x + 1
```

The expression defining `adder1` is similar:

```
add(counter)(_)
```

It expands to:

```
a => add(counter)(a)
```

This is a function value, so the evaluation of argument `counter` is deferred until `adder1` is evaluated.

The kind of expression that defines `adder2` is different:

```
val adder2 = add(counter) _
```

This expression *is* an example of a partially applied function, since the parameter b of method `add` is not supplied. Thus *eta expansion*[2] takes place to convert the method into a function of the remaining parameters. This entails creating *fresh values* for every supplied method argument, which, as a result, causes the arguments to be evaluated eagerly. In the case of `adder2`, the compiler generates something along these lines behind the scenes:

```
val adder2 = {
  val fresh = counter()
  a => add(fresh)(a)
}
```

---

[1] Odersky, *The Scala Language Specification*, Section 6.23. [Ode14]
[2] Odersky, *The Scala Language Specification*, Section 6.26.5. [Ode14]

Hence, the crucial difference between `adder1` and `adder2` has to do with the evaluation of argument `counter`. In `adder1`, `counter` will be evaluated each time `adder1` is used. In `adder2`, `counter` is evaluated once and will not be evaluated again when the function is called.

Eta expansion

Eta expansion[a] is the operation of automatically coercing a method into an equivalent function.[b] Given the method:

```scala
def foo[A, B](a: A): B
```

eta expansion is performed in either of the following conditions:[c]

- an underscore is given in lieu of an argument list:

```scala
val f = foo _ // f is inferred as A => B
```

- no argument list is provided and a function type is expected:

```scala
val f: A => B = foo
```

---

[a]Odersky, *The Scala Language Specification*, Section 6.26.5. [Ode14]

[b]Gleichmann, "Functional Scala: Turning Methods into Functions." [Gle11]

[c]Zaugg, "In Scala, why can't I partially apply a function without explicitly specifying its argument types?" [Zau10a]

Now let's walk through the program. In the first three lines, the value of x is 0:

```scala
var x = 0
def counter() = { x += 1; x }
def add(a: Int)(b: Int) = a + b
```

In the next line, the `adder1` function value is defined but `counter` is not evaluated, so x is still 0:

```scala
val adder1 = add(counter)(_)
```

Method `counter` is executed for the first time in the next line, when `adder2` is initialized:

```
val adder2 = add(counter) _
```

This, therefore, increments x to 1. At this point, parameter a of method add for adder1 is bound to value 1. After that, the current value of x is printed, which is still 1 at this point:

```
println("x = " + x)
```

The subsequent line applies adder1 to 10, executing counter along the way and incrementing x to 2:

```
println(adder1(10))
```

Consequently, this prints 12, and the next statement reveals that x equals 2. The following line then applies adder2 to 10:

```
println(adder2(10))
```

At the time function adder2 was created, counter evaluated to 1. This call to adder2 adds 10 to 1 to produce 11. And finally, the last line prints 2, because the value of x has not since it was last printed.

Therefore, the correct answer is number 1:

```
scala> println("x = " + x)
x = 1
scala> println(adder1(10))
12
scala> println("x = " + x)
x = 2
scala> println(adder2(10))
11
scala> println("x = " + x)
x = 2
```

Every subsequent invocation of adder2 will return the same result, unlike invoking adder1, which will keep incrementing x:

```
scala> println(adder1(10))
13
scala> println(adder2(10))
11
```

Discussion

It is worth noting a couple of points about this program. First, the use of vars does not reflect idiomatic Scala style. Even though Scala supports mutable state, it encourages a functional style of programming, *i.e.*, preferring vals and immutability.

Second, the surprising behavior is manifested only in side-effecting code. The side effect inside counter, x += 1, is what makes this program difficult to reason about. This is one of the drawbacks of imperative programming: when functions are passed around and manipulated, it is hard to know when and how many times they will be called. The outcome is more predictable when calling a function that has no effect on the outside world.

Lastly, a common error is to try to construct adder with the intent of partially applying method add, but without explicitly writing the underscore symbol, like this:

```scala
val adder3 = add(counter)
```

That, unfortunately, results in a compiler error:

```scala
scala> val adder3 = add(counter)
<console>:10: error: missing arguments for method add;
  follow this method with `_' if you want to treat it
  as a partially applied function
        val adder3 = add(counter)
                     ^
```

The reason for this error is that the compiler is not explicitly expecting adder3 to be a function value (*i.e.*, of type Function1[Int, Int]). If you specify the type of adder3, the compiler performs eta expansion without complaining:

```scala
scala> val adder3: Int => Int = add(counter)
adder3:Int => Int => <function1>
```

This comes in handy when a method is expecting a function as an argument. For example, consider the fold method on a List[A]:

```scala
def fold[A1 >: A](z: A1)(op: (A1, A1) => A1): A1
```

Imagine you want to fold using a sum operation defined as:

```
def sum(a: Int, b: Int) = a + b
```

You can explicitly pass sum with the underscore:

```
List(1, 2, 3).fold(0)(sum _)
```

But you can also omit it:

```
List(1, 2, 3).fold(0)(sum)
```

In short, Scala allows you to leave off the underscore after a method name when it knows the expected type is a function, and the type of the function is consistent with the signature of the method.

Familiarize yourself with anonymous and partially applied functions as well as the other uses of the underscore symbol. In general, try to avoid writing code that readers can easily misinterpret.

Puzzler 16

One Bound, Two to Go

Through currying, Scala allows methods to be defined with multiple parameter lists. Consider the following two method definitions:

```
def regular(x: Int, y: Int, z: Int) = x + y + z
def curried(x: Int)(y: Int)(z: Int) = x + y + z
```

Both methods compute the same result when given identical values for their corresponding arguments:

```
scala> regular(1, 2, 3)
res0: Int = 6

scala> curried(1)(2)(3)
res1: Int = 6
```

Despite this similarity, the curried method is fundamentally different from the regular one: the invocation of curried represents *three* consecutive function invocations.[1]

Scala also supports default arguments, which significantly reduces the need for method overloading. Furthermore, by combining default arguments with named arguments, a subset of arguments can be provided when invoking a method, in any order. This allows you to invoke the method more flexibly and makes the call site more robust against refactoring errors.

The following program defines a curried method with two parameter lists. Default argument values are stipulated for the parameters in the second list. What is the result of executing the following code in the Scala REPL?

---

[1]The compiler can turn these consecutive invocations into a single method call if all arguments are provided.

91

```
def invert(v3: Int)(v2: Int = 2, v1: Int = 1) {
  println(v1 + ", " + v2 + ", " + v3)
}

val invert3 = invert(3) _

invert3(v1 = 2)
invert3(v1 = 2, v2 = 1)
```

Possibilities

1. Prints:

   ```
   2, 2, 3
   2, 1, 3
   ```

2. The first invocation of invert3 fails to compile, and the second one prints:

   ```
   1, 2, 3
   ```

3. The first invocation of invert3 fails to compile, and the second one prints:

   ```
   2, 1, 3
   ```

4. The first invocation of invert3 fails to compile, and the second one prints:

   ```
   2, 2, 3
   ```

Explanation

The type of `invert3` is a function type, because only the first parameter list is provided when `invert` is invoked:

```
scala> val invert3 = invert(3) _
invert3: (Int, Int) => Unit = <function2>
```

Function `invert3` takes two arguments of type `Int`, but the first invocation supplies only one: `v1 = 2`. Parameter `v2` has a default value of 2, so you might assume that the first invocation of `invert3` would print:

```
2, 2, 3
```

And you would then expect the second invocation to print:

```
2, 1, 3
```

Let's verify:

```
scala> invert3(v1 = 2)
<console>:10: error: not enough arguments for method apply:
  (v1: Int, v2: Int)Unit in trait Function2.
Unspecified value parameter v2.
             invert3(v1 = 2)
                    ^

scala> invert3(v1 = 2, v2 = 1)
1, 2, 3
```

So, not the output of the first candidate answer. It turns out the correct answer is number 2! What is going on?

The compiler error gives us a hint: the answer lies in understanding how function types are actually implemented. As stated in *The Scala Language Specification*,[2] they represent shorthands for anonymous class types that have an `apply` method, defined as follows:[3]

```
// abstract apply method of Function2[T1, T2, R]
def apply(v1: T1, v2: T2): R
```

---

[2] Odersky, *The Scala Language Specification*, Section 3.2.9. [Ode14]
[3] See the Scaladoc for `Function2`. [EPF]

Therefore, the original program is expanded during compilation to something along these lines:

```scala
def invert(v3: Int)(v2: Int = 2, v1: Int = 1) {
  println(v1 + ", " + v2 + ", " + v3)
}
def invert3 = new Function2[Int, Int, Unit] {
  def apply(v1: Int, v2: Int): Unit = invert(3)(v1, v2)
}
invert3.apply(v1 = 2)
invert3.apply(v1 = 2, v2 = 1)
```

Two things stand out about the signature of method `apply`. First, there are
no default values for the method parameters. As a consequence, the first
invocation of `invert3` results in a compiler error, since only one argument,
v1 = 2, is being passed.

Second, the parameters are actually called v1 and v2. Had the `invert`
method used different names for its parameters, even the second invocation
of `invert3` would have failed to compile. The parameters of the `apply`
method on *all* `Function2` instances have such names; there is no link to the
parameter names of the initial `invert` method.

Finally, because `invert3` happens to have the same parameter names,
but in the reverse order, the second invocation prints:

```scala
scala> invert3(v1 = 2, v2 = 1)
1, 2, 3
```

Even though you might *think* that the named arguments pertain to `invert`,
they actually refer to the parameters of the `apply` method. More precisely,
parameter v1 of `apply`, which corresponds to v2 of `invert`, is set to 2.
Likewise, parameter v2 of method `apply`, corresponding to v1 of `invert`, is
set to 1.

Discussion

You may wonder about the rationale for defining parameters of the `invert`
method in separate parameter lists. There are several reasons you might
decide to define method parameters in such a manner, rather than using a

single parameter list. First, you can refer to the parameters of a previous parameter list when defining default arguments:

```
def area(x: Int)(y: Int = x) = x * y
```

Multiple parameter lists can also facilitate type inference, because types inferred in earlier parameter lists need not be specified. Take the foldLeft method from Scala's collection library as an example:[4]

```
def foldLeft[B](z: B)(op: (B, A) => B): B
// no need to specify Int for B
Seq("I", "II", "III").foldLeft(0)(_ + _.length)
```

Multiple parameter lists allow you to have both implicit and non-implicit parameters:

```
def maxBy[B](f: A => B)(implicit cmp: Ordering[B]): A
```

And they let you define fluent APIs that use curly braces instead of parentheses to surround a parameter list:[5]

```
def benchmark(times: Int)(block: => Unit): Unit
benchmark(10000) {
  ...
}
```

One final benefit of currying illustrated by this puzzler is that multiple parameter lists can allow partially applied functions to be expressed concisely. For example, imagine that method invert were declared using a single parameter list:

```
def invert(v3: Int, v2: Int = 2, v1: Int = 1) {
  println(v1 + ", " + v2 + ", " + v3)
}
```

You could not apply this form of invert to only one argument using the following syntax:

---

[4] See Puzzler 6 for an additional discussion of type parameters that occur in multiple parameter lists.

[5] For a more detailed discussion of curly braces versus parentheses, see Puzzler 35.

```
scala> def invert3 = invert(3) _
<console>:8: error: _ must follow method; cannot follow Unit
       def invert3 = invert(3) _
                            ^
```

You would need to provide underscores and a type ascription for *each* missing argument:

```
scala> def invert3 = invert(3, _: Int, _: Int)
invert3: (Int, Int) => Unit
```

When it comes to methods with single parameter lists, the only case where you can get away with not specifying argument types is when you pass an underscore for all arguments:

```
scala> def invert3 = invert(_, _, _)
invert3: (Int, Int, Int) => Unit
```

Bear in mind that when you are invoking a partially applied function, named arguments do not resolve against the original method, but against a generated function object. You can avoid problems by steering clear of parameter names used by Scala's function traits.

Puzzler 17

Implicitly Surprising

The ability to create and pass around partially applied functions helps you to move from specific to more general and reusable functionality. Instead of a method that increments a value by two, for instance, we can write a more generally applicable add method and specialize it for our use case:

```scala
def add(x: Int)(y: Int) = x + y
def addTo2 = add(2) _

scala> addTo2(3)
res2: Int = 5
```

Scala also supports implicits, which, among other things, allows you to pick up arguments from the context rather than passing them explicitly to methods and functions.

How do these two play together? What is the result of executing the following code in the REPL?

```scala
implicit val z1 = 2
def add(x: Int)(y: Int)(implicit z: Int) = x + y + z
def addTo(n: Int) = add(n) _

implicit val z2 = 3
val addTo1 = addTo(1)
addTo1(2)
addTo1(2)(3)
```

Possibilities

1. Prints:

   5
   6

2. Prints:

   6
   6

3. The first invocation of addTo1 prints:

   5

   and the second fails to compile.

4. The first invocation of addTo1 fails to compile, and the second prints:

   6

Explanation

You may wonder whether add's implicit parameter becomes an implicit parameter of the partially applied function that is returned by addTo, or whether it is somehow "converted" to a regular parameter list. If addTo1 has an implicit parameter, or if the compiler instead attempts to resolve the implicit inside the invocation of addTo, will you run into problems with ambiguous implicit values for z?

Neither, in fact. The correct answer is number 3:

```scala
scala> addTo1(2)
res0: Int = 5

scala> addTo1(2)(3)
<console>:12: error: Int does not take parameters
              addTo1(2)(3)
                       ^
```

What happened to method add's implicit parameter? And how was a clash between the two ambiguous implicit values z1 and z2 avoided?

To address the first question, first observe that the type signature of addTo1 shows that it is a function of *one*, not two parameters:

```scala
scala> val addTo1 = addTo(1)
addTo1: Int => Int = <function1>
```

In other words, while add's regular parameter y is also a parameter of the eta-expanded function addTo1, the implicit parameter z is *not*. Instead, the implicit is resolved at the moment *eta expansion*[1] is applied in the body of method addTo.

How does the compiler choose the implicit value z1, however? After all, by the time addTo is invoked in the expression val addTo1 = addTo(1), both z1 and z2 are in scope.

The explanation is straightforward: the implicit is resolved by the compiler when method addTo is compiled, not when it is later invoked.[2] At that point, the only implicit in scope is z1. The method addTo effectively becomes:

```scala
def add(x: Int)(y: Int) = x + y + 2
def addToWithResolvedImplicit(n: Int) = add(n) _
```

This behaves in the same way as the original addTo method:

```scala
scala> val addTo1WithResolvedImplicit =
          addToWithResolvedImplicit(1)
addTo1WithResolvedImplicit: Int => Int = <function1>

scala> addTo1WithResolvedImplicit(2)
res2: Int = 5

scala> addTo1WithResolvedImplicit(2)(3)
<console>:12: error: Int does not take parameters
          addTo1WithResolvedImplicit(2)(3)
                                        ^
```

---

[1] Eta expansion is discussed in more detail in Puzzler 15.
[2] Odersky, *The Scala Language Specification*, Section 7.2. [Ode14]

Discussion

If the implicit values z1 and z2 were both in scope when addTo is declared, the code would indeed fail to compile:

```
implicit val z1 = 2
implicit val z2 = 3
def add(x: Int)(y: Int)(implicit z: Int) = x + y + z
scala> def addTo(n: Int) = add(n) _
<console>:10: error: ambiguous implicit values:
 both value z1 of type => Int
 and value z2 of type => Int
 match expected type Int
        def addTo(n: Int) = add(n) _
                                   ^
```

Resolution of the implicit parameter cannot be prevented using eta expansion, but you can retain z as a parameter by avoiding eta expansion entirely—just explicitly construct an anonymous function to return:

```
def addToReturnAnonFun(n: Int) =
  (y: Int) => (z: Int) => add(n)(y)(z)
scala> val addTo1ReturnAnonFun = addToReturnAnonFun(1)
addTo1ReturnAnonFun: Int => (Int => Int) = <function1>

scala> addTo1ReturnAnonFun(2)
res0: Int => Int = <function1>

scala> addTo1ReturnAnonFun(2)(3)
res1: Int = 6
```

The addToReturnAnonFun method creates and returns a curried function with two parameter lists, consistent with the two parameter lists (y) and (z) of the add method. If you try to use placeholder syntax to make the definition of the anonymous function more concise, you end up with a function with two parameters, *not* a curried function:

100

Anonymous Functions and Implicit Parameters

You might reasonably assume that implicit parameters are resolved during eta expansion because anonymous functions simply do not support implicit parameters. In fact they do.[a]

The semantics of implicit parameters in anonymous functions is slightly different, however, from that of implicit parameters in methods: the compiler will *not* automatically resolve them—they need to be explicitly specified when the anonymous function is invoked.

How do implicit parameters in anonymous functions differ from regular ones, then? The purpose of the `implicit` keyword is to make the value eligible for implicit resolution in the *body* of the anonymous function. A short example can demonstrate this:

```
def iNeedAnImplicit(implicit n: Int) = n + 1

scala> val anonFun = { x: Int => y: Int =>
         x + y + iNeedAnImplicit }
<console>:8: error: could not find implicit value for
  parameter n: Int
          val anonFun = { x: Int => y: Int =>
          x + y + iNeedAnImplicit }
                      ^

scala> val anonFunWithImplicitParam = { x: Int =>
         implicit y: Int => x + y + iNeedAnImplicit }
anonFunWithImplicitParam:
  Int => (Int => Int) = <function1>

implicit val z = 2

scala> anonFunWithImplicitParam(1)(2)
res4: Int = 6

// the compiler will not supply the implicit argument
scala> anonFunWithImplicitParam(1)
res5: Int => Int = <function1>
```

---

[a]Odersky, *The Scala Language Specification*, Section 6.23. [Ode14]

```
def addToReturnPlaceholderAnonFun(n: Int) =
  add(n)(_: Int)(_: Int)
```

```
scala> val addTo1ReturnPlaceholderAnonFun =
         addToReturnPlaceholderAnonFun(1)
addTo1ReturnPlaceholderAnonFun: (Int, Int) => Int = <function2>
```

In both cases, the second parameter of the partially applied function is not implicit, and must be explicitly provided when invoking the function.

 Bear in mind that, during eta expansion, implicit parameters are resolved. They are not parameters of the resulting function value.

Puzzler 18

Information Overload

Overloaded methods are a common way of providing functions that can be applied to various combinations of arguments. Some care is required here, since new versions of an overloaded method can mean that the compiler needs to distinguish between multiple applicable versions where the method is called. If the compiler cannot identify a single, most applicable method, compilation will fail:

```scala
def foo(n: Int, a: Any) {
  println(s"n: ${n}, a: ${a}") }
scala> foo(1, 2)
n: 1, a: 2
object A {
  def foo(n: Int, a: Any) {
    println(s"n: ${n}, a: ${a}") }
  def foo(a: Any, n: Int) {
    println(s"a: ${a}, n: ${n}") }
}
scala> A.foo(1, 2)
<console>:10: error: ambiguous reference to
  overloaded definition,
both method foo in object A of type (a: Any, n: Int)Unit
and  method foo in object A of type (n: Int, a: Any)Unit
match argument types (Int,Int)
          A.foo(1, 2)
            ^
```

In the following example, the method signatures appear to be designed to prevent such ambiguous method calls. What is the result of executing the following code?

```
object Oh {
  def overloadA(u: Unit) = "I accept a Unit"
  def overloadA(u: Unit, n: Nothing) =
      "I accept a Unit and Nothing"
  def overloadB(n: Unit) = "I accept a Unit"
  def overloadB(n: Nothing) = "I accept Nothing"
}
println(Oh overloadA 99)
println(Oh overloadB 99)
```

Possibilities

1. The first statement fails to compile and the second prints:

   ```
   I accept Nothing
   ```

2. The first statements prints:

   ```
   I accept a Unit
   ```

   and the second fails to compile.

3. Both statements fail to compile.

4. Prints:

   ```
   I accept a Unit
   I accept a Unit
   ```

Explanation

Since Int does not inherit from Unit, you may suspect that either the first or both statements fail to compile. Or you may assume that the compiler *is* able to treat the argument 99 as a Unit, and deduce that "I accept a Unit" would be printed in both cases. But surely the compiler cannot accept Int as a Unit in the first case, but *reject* in the second?

Oh yes, it can. The correct answer is indeed number 2:

```
scala> println(Oh overloadA 99)
<console>:9: warning: a pure expression does nothing
   in statement position; you may be omitting necessary
   parentheses
            println(Oh overloadA 99)
                          ^

I accept a Unit
scala> println(Oh overloadB 99)
<console>:9: error: overloaded method value overloadB
     with alternatives:
  (n: Nothing)String <and>
  (n: Unit)String
 cannot be applied to (Int)
            println(Oh overloadB 99)
                          ^
```

To be clear: the compiler is not failing here because an overloaded method that is *also* applicable has been added, resulting in an ambiguous reference. The overloadB(n: Nothing) method does not accept an Int argument. What is instead happening here is that a method that was applicable now no longer applies because of an overloaded method that *also* does not apply at the point where the method is called.

For an explanation of this seemingly extraordinary behavior, you must dive into the details of Scala's overloading resolution.[1] If an identifier, such as overloadA, refers to multiple members of a class, Scala applies a two-stage algorithm to determine, if possible, the appropriate member to invoke.

In the first stage, the compiler compares the "shapes" of the member declarations with the invocation to see which of the possible alternatives "looks

---

[1]Odersky, *The Scala Language Specification*, Section 6.26.3. [Ode14]

right." Roughly speaking, the compiler looks at the number of parameters of each overloaded alternative and compares these with the invocation.[2] If precisely one alternative is feasible, it is chosen.

This convenient shortcut, which allows the compiler to avoid potentially expensive type-based resolution, is sufficient in the first case: only one of the alternatives for overloadA has the "right shape" (*i.e.*, takes one argument), so this option is chosen by the compiler. One hurdle remains: how to get the Int argument 99 to match with the expected Unit type?

Here, one of Scala's *value conversions*[3] comes into play. These implicit conversions can be applied by the compiler to convert a value type to a different expected type, if needed. In this case, *value discarding* is applied: the compiler converts the Int to the expected Unit type by embedding it in the term { 99; () }. This, incidentally, causes the observed compiler warning.

In the case of overloadB, however, shape-based resolution is *not* sufficient to determine a unique alternative, since both options take one argument. The compiler therefore proceeds to the *second* stage of overloading resolution, which attempts to find precisely one option with the most specific parameter type.[4]

Herein lies the explanation for the observed behavior, because the first step of this type-based resolution stage is to determine the types of all of the supplied arguments *without considering the expected types of the possible methods to be called*. In this case, the process is equivalent to evaluating val arg = 99 (*i.e.*, as opposed to val arg: Unit = 99) and looking at the resulting type. This seems reasonable enough, since at this point the compiler does not yet *know* which of the methods will be invoked, so it also does not know what the expected types will be.

The argument 99 is thus determined to be an Int, and now the compiler proceeds to try to identify a most specific overloaded method to which the argument can be applied. But Int inherits neither from Unit nor from Nothing, so *none* of the alternatives are applicable!

Furthermore, the value conversion, which in the case of overloadA turns 99 into a Unit, is *also* not available, since it only applies *if the expected type of the value is known*. But since the compiler has not been able to identify a most specific method to call, it also does not know the expected type that

[2]Odersky, *The Scala Language Specification*, Section 6.26.3. [Ode14]

[3]Odersky, *The Scala Language Specification*, Section 6.26.1. [Ode14]

[4]Odersky, *The Scala Language Specification*, Section 6.26.3. [Ode14]

would be required. Ergo: *neither* of the two alternatives are applicable, so the code fails to compile.

> ### The Magnet Pattern
>
> As demonstrated here, method overloading in Scala has certain drawbacks.[a] While not applicable to the code example in this puzzler, the Magnet Pattern[b] provides an interesting alternative. In the Magnet Pattern, multiple overloaded method definitions are replaced by a single method and a set of implicit conversions for each supported combination of argument types.
>
> ---
> [a]Zaugg, "Why 'avoid method overloading'?". [Zau10b]
> [b]Mathias, "The Magnet Pattern." [Mat12]

Discussion

A variation of this problem that is likely to occur in production code involves methods with empty parameter lists. These can be converted to () => T function types via *eta expansion* where such a type is expected, but this conversion cannot be taken into account by the compiler during a type-based overloading resolution:

```scala
object Oh2 {
  def nonOverloadedA(f: () => Any) =
    "I accept a no-arg function"
  def overloadedA(f: () => Any) =
    "I accept a no-arg function"
  def overloadedA(n: Nothing) = "I accept Nothing"
}

def emptyParamList() = 99

scala> Oh2 nonOverloadedA emptyParamList
res0: String = I accept a no-arg function

scala> Oh2 overloadedA emptyParamList
<console>:10: error: overloaded method value overloadedA
    with alternatives:
```

```
(n: Nothing)String <and>
(f: () => Any)String
cannot be applied to (Int)
            Oh2 overloadedA emptyParamList
              ^
```

What to do about this potential problem? Since the error occurs only where the method is *invoked*, you as the code's author have few options beyond avoiding overloaded methods of the same shape entirely. As a user, there is also little you can do other than to keep a keen eye out for implicit type conversions: unfortunately, there are currently no compiler options that flag applications of these automatically.

1. Watch out for type conversions inserted by the compiler that depend on the expected type, such as value discarding, view application (*i.e.*, applying implicit conversions), and eta expansion. These conversions may no longer be applicable if overloaded versions of the invoked method are added.

2. Be aware that defining an overloaded method with the *same shape* as an existing alternative can cause calling code to fail to compile regardless of the parameter types of the new method.

Puzzler 19

What's in a Name?

Relying on the precise order of items in a parameter list is fragile, especially if parameters are of the same type:

```scala
def inEcosystem(predator: String, prey: String) {
  println(s"${predator} eat ${prey}")
}
scala> inEcosystem("cats", "mice")
cats eat mice
def inEcosystem(prey: String, predator: String) {
  println(s"${prey} are eaten by ${predator}")
}
// no idea that the definition has changed...
scala> inEcosystem("cats", "mice")
cats are eaten by mice
scala> inEcosystem(predator = "cats", prey = "mice")
mice are eaten by cats
```

Scala also supports default arguments,[1] making it easy to write versatile functions and provide for common use cases without a combinatorial explosion of overloaded methods:

```scala
object MakeSequences {
  def mkSeq(end: Int, start: Int = 1, step: Int = 1) = ...
```

---

[1] See Puzzler 16 for a more detailed discussion of default arguments.

109

```
// rather than...
def mkSeq2(end: Int, start: Int, step: Int) = ...
def mkSeq2(end: Int, start: Int) = mkSeq2(end, start, 1)
def mkSeq2(end: Int) = mkSeq2(end, 1, 1)
}
```

This puzzler uses a combination of named and default arguments to invoke an overridden method. What is the result of executing the following code in the REPL?

```
class SimpleAdder {
  def add(x: Int = 1, y: Int = 2): Int = x + y
}
class AdderWithBonus extends SimpleAdder {
  override def add(y: Int = 3, x: Int = 4): Int =
    super.add(x, y) + 10
}
val adder: SimpleAdder = new AdderWithBonus
adder add (y = 0)
adder add 0
```

Possibilities

1. Prints:

   ```
   14
   12
   ```

2. Prints:

   ```
   14
   14
   ```

3. Prints:

   ```
   13
   14
   ```

4. Prints:

```
11
12
```

Explanation

You may wonder whether declaring adder as a SimpleAdder somehow causes the default values of *its* add method to be applied, printing 11 and 12. Alternatively, if the overriding version in AdderWithBonus is chosen, surely 14 and 14 would then be displayed?

Not so. The correct answer is number 3:

```
scala> adder add (y = 0)
res10: Int = 13

scala> adder add 0
res11: Int = 14
```

Given the possible values, the only way this outcome can be achieved is if the default value for x in class AdderWithBonus is used in both cases, *i.e.*, even when y = 0 is specified.

How can this be? To understand the result, you need to examine how Scala handles named and default arguments.[2] Since the JVM does not support these natively, the compiler needs to transform an invocation with such arguments into a "regular" call in which all arguments are passed in the order required by the function definition.

The compiler accomplishes this by defining a variable for each parameter required by the function and assigning the value of all provided arguments, positional and named, to the appropriate variables. For all other parameters, the compiler invokes special "default methods" that are automatically added to classes that define default parameter values.[3] The target method is then invoked with *all* arguments. In the second statement, adder add 0, this turns into the following:

---

[2] Odersky, *The Scala Language Specification*, Section 6.6.1. [Ode14]
[3] Odersky, *The Scala Language Specification*, Section 4.6. [Ode14]

111

```
{
  val x$1 = 0 // arg at position 0
  val x$2 = adder.add$default$2
  adder.add(x$1, x$2)
}
res12: Int = 14
```

In the case of `adder` add (y = 0), an additional step is required. The compiler needs to rearrange the variables so that the correct values appear at the expected positions. It does this using the only information available when the call is compiled: the method definition of the type of the value being invoked.

Since adder's type is `SimpleAdder`—not `AdderWithBonus`, which is its *runtime* type—this means that the compiler moves the value 0 to the position of parameter y *on SimpleAdder's definition of add*:

```
{
  val x$1 = 0 // named arg for 'y'
  val x$2 = adder.add$default$1
  adder.add(x$2, x$1) // matches order in SimpleAdder.add
}
res13: Int = 13
```

The values of the default arguments are determined at runtime by invoking default methods—here, `add$default$1`. The new defaults specified in `AdderWithBonus` cause the compiler to generate overrides for the default methods in `SimpleAdder`. As a result, the default parameter values *defined for AdderWithBonus*, the runtime type of adder, are used.

Discussion

If the type of adder is not explicitly specified, the result is less surprising:

```
val adder2 = new AdderWithBonus

scala> adder2 add (y = 0)
res14: Int = 14

scala> adder2 add 0
res15: Int = 14
```

112

Obviously, the easiest way to avoid the scenario in the main code sample is to ensure that the order of parameters in AdderWithBonus.add matches those of the overridden version:

```scala
class SimpleAdder {
  def add(x: Int = 1, y: Int = 2): Int = x + y
}
class AdderWithBonus2 extends SimpleAdder {
  override def add(x: Int = 4, y: Int = 3): Int =
    super.add(x, y) + 10
}
val adder3: SimpleAdder = new AdderWithBonus2
scala> adder3 add (y = 0)
res16: Int = 14

scala> adder3 add 0
res17: Int = 13

val adder4 = new AdderWithBonus2
scala> adder4 add (y = 0)
res18: Int = 14

scala> adder4 add 0
res19: Int = 13
```

1. Where possible, preserve the parameter order when overriding methods.

2. When using named and default arguments, remember (to paraphrase Josh Suereth): "Names are compile time; values are runtime."

Puzzler 20

Irregular Expressions

You may have heard the old joke: "A developer has a problem and decides to solve it with a regular expression. Now they have *two* problems." Regular expressions can indeed get complicated quickly. But they are also very powerful, and can be extremely useful if used judiciously.

Scala's `scala.util.matching.Regex` class provides utility functions for regular expressions. Its `findAllIn` method returns a `MatchIterator` that iterates over all the occurrences of the regular expression in a string:

```
scala> for (reMatch <- "l".r.findAllIn("I love Scala"))
         println(reMatch)
l
l
```

In the next example, a `MatchIterator` is twice queried for the index of the first regular expression match in a string using the `start` method. In one case, we also trace the call. What is the result of executing this code:

```
def traceIt[T <: Iterator[_]](it: T) = {
  println(s"TRACE: using iterator '${it}'")
  it
}
val msg = "I love Scala"
println("First match index: " +
  traceIt("a".r.findAllIn(msg)).start)
println("First match index: " +
  "a".r.findAllIn(msg).start)
```

Possibilities

1. Prints:

```
TRACE: using iterator 'non-empty iterator'
First match index: 9
First match index: 9
```

2. Both statements throw a runtime exception.

3. The first statement prints:

```
TRACE: using iterator 'non-empty iterator'
First match index: 9
```

and the second throws a runtime exception.

4. The first statement throws a runtime exception, and the second prints:

```
First match index: 9
```

Explanation

Even though the regular expression, "a", certainly looks as though it should match the string, "I love Scala", you may wonder whether something could be happening that causes no matches to be found. Or you may suspect that, somehow, simply printing the iterator in the trace method causes things to go wrong. Otherwise, surely both statements should print that the first occurrence of "a" in "I love Scala" is indeed at index 9?

Not so. In fact, the correct answer is number 3:

```
scala> println("First match index: " +
         traceIt("a".r.findAllIn(msg)).start)
TRACE: using iterator 'non-empty iterator'
First match index: 9

scala> println("First match index: " +
         "a".r.findAllIn(msg).start)
```

```
java.lang.IllegalStateException: No match available
   at java.util.regex.Matcher.end(Matcher.java:389)
   at scala.util.matching.Regex$MatchIterator.end(
      Regex.scala:667)
   ...
```

Huh? The debugging method doesn't "stay out of the way," it actually enables the statement to succeed? What does it do beyond simply printing the iterator's string representation?

Well, nothing! But printing—or more accurately—*generating* the string representation of a `MatchIterator` has a hidden side effect. This effect allows the statement with the debugging call to succeed, while the "untraced" version fails.

The key point is that, as the stack trace of the failed statement indicates, Scala's regex support builds on Java's `java.util.regex` package. In particular, Scala's `MatchIterator` is backed by a `java.util.regex.Matcher`, which has the following characteristic:[1]

> The explicit state of a matcher is initially undefined; attempting to query any part of it before a successful match will cause an `IllegalStateException` to be thrown.

Before you can call `start`, `end`, or any other method on `MatchIterator` that delegates to the underlying `Matcher`, you therefore first need to initialize that matcher! Invoking `MatchIterator`'s `toString` method fortuitously achieves this since `Iterator`'s `toString` implementation, which `MatchIterator` inherits, calls `hasNext`. This in turn attempts to find a match and initializes the matcher.

Discussion

Obviously, relying on an implementation detail of the `Iterator.toString` method is not a particularly smart strategy. In any case, you are not usually interested in the string representation when using a `MatchIterator`. Calling `hasNext`—or, if you know the iterator will be non-empty, `next()`—is a more reliable approach:

---

[1] See the Javadoc for `java.util.regex.Matcher`. [Ora]

```
scala> { // without a block the REPL will call toString
        val mi = "a".r.findAllIn(msg)
        mi.hasNext // initialize the matcher
        println("First match index: " + mi.start)
      }
First match index: 9
```

If you are planning to iterate over the matches using a for expression or by invoking foreach, map, *etc.*, you don't need to do anything. These method invocations will initialize the matcher for you.

You can avoid the problem entirely by using Regex's findAllMatchIn method instead. This converts the iterator to an Iterator[Match] and is equivalent to calling MatchIterator's matchData method, which converts the iterator to an Iterator[Match]. In both cases, you simply cannot call "dangerous" methods such as start without first iterating to a match, which initializes the underlying matcher:

```
scala> {
        val mi = "a".r.findAllMatchIn(msg)
        println("First match index: " + mi.next().start)
      }
First match index: 9
scala> {
        val mi = "a".r.findAllIn(msg).matchData
        println("First match index: " + mi.next().start)
      }
First match index: 9
```

Prefer Regex's findAllMatchIn method to findAllIn, or convert the MatchIterator returned by findAllIn to an Iterator[Match] by calling the MatchIterator.matchData method.

Puzzler 21

I Can Has Padding?

Scala provides an incremental string builder that shares the same name as, and therefore hides, java.lang.StringBuilder. Scala's StringBuilder is similar to Java's for the most part, differing mainly where providing the same methods as the Java class would conflict with the Scala collections library. And like java.lang.StringBuilder, Scala's StringBuilder is not synchronized, leaving you to handle thread safety by other means.

The following program demonstrates a StringBuilder in action. What does it do?

```scala
implicit class Padder(val sb: StringBuilder) extends AnyVal {
  def pad2(width: Int) = {
    1 to width - sb.length foreach { sb += '*' }
    sb
  }
}
// length == 14
val greeting = new StringBuilder("Hello, kitteh!")
println(greeting pad2 20)

// length == 9
val farewell = new StringBuilder("U go now.")
println(farewell pad2 20)
```

119

Possibilities

1. Prints:

   ```
   Hello, kitteh!******
   U go now.***********
   ```

2. The first statement prints:

   ```
   Hello, kitteh!*
   ```

   and the second one throws an exception.

3. The first statement throws an exception and the second one prints:

   ```
   U go now.***********
   ```

4. Fails to compile.

Explanation

The code looks simple enough. It consists of an implicit value class[1] that transparently enriches StringBuilder with the pad2 method. The pad2 method pads a string with a specified number of asterisks. The method is then invoked twice.

Although the first answer may appear most plausible, it is, in fact, not the right one. Instead, the correct answer is number 2:

```
scala> println(greeting pad2 20)
Hello, kitteh!*

scala> println(farewell pad2 20)
java.lang.StringIndexOutOfBoundsException:
    String index out of range: 10
  at j.l.StringBuilder.charAt(StringBuilder.java:55)
  at s.c.m.StringBuilder.apply(StringBuilder.scala:114)
  at s.c.m.StringBuilder.apply(StringBuilder.scala:28)
```

---

[1] Suereth, "Implicit Classes." [Sue]

> **Value Classes**
>
> You may have noticed that `Padder` is a subclass of `AnyVal`. This makes
> it a *value class*. Value classes reduce runtime overhead by avoiding
> object allocation. Extension methods, such as `pad2`, are a typical use
> case for value classes.[a]
>
> ---
>
> [a]Harrah, "Value Classes and Universal Traits." [Har]

```
at s.c.i.Range.foreach(Range.scala:141)
at Padder$.pad2$extension(<console>:9)
...
```

As the saying goes, the truth is in the details, so take a closer look at the implementation of the `pad2` method. The expression, `1 to width - sb.length`,
is a `Range`, and its `foreach` method accepts a function as a argument:

```
final def foreach(f: (A) => Unit): Unit
```

It does not seem as if we are passing a function, though, as the `+=` method—
essentially an alias for the `StringBuilder.append` method—returns the
`StringBuilder` itself. The code does compile, however, so that can only
mean that `StringBuilder` is itself a function. A look at the Scaladoc confirms that Scala's `StringBuilder` inherits from `Function1`, which brings
you to the `apply` method of `StringBuilder`:

```
def apply(index: Int): Char
```

Equivalent to charAt.

returns   the element of this growable collection at index
idx, where 0 indicates the first element.

Now things start to make sense. It is *not* the expression `sb += '*'`
that is executed on each iteration of `foreach`. Instead, `+=` is called *once*
when the argument to `foreach` is being evaluated! In fact, it is the resulting
`StringBuilder` whose `apply` method is invoked each time, retrieving the
character at the given index, but not assigning it to anything. Method `pad2`
is actually equivalent to the following:

121

```
def pad2(width: Int) = {
  val appendedSb = sb += '*'
  // apply calls charAt
  1 to width - sb.length foreach appendedSb.apply
  sb
}
```

In both cases, 20 is passed as width to pad2, which runs without errors for the "Hello, kitteh!" string, as the maximum index passed to charAt is 6. The value of the StringBuilder (the input string plus one padding asterisk) is then printed. The second string, "U go now.", is shorter, so the range stretches to 11, which is greater than the length of the "U go now." string. Method charAt is eventually called with index 10, which results in a StringIndexOutOfBoundsException.

Discussion

To correctly pad the string, as intended, all that's required is to explicitly specify the function literal:

```
def pad2(width: Int) = {
  1 to width - sb.length foreach { _ => sb += '*' }
  sb
}
```

This happens automatically if you use a for expression, which the compiler translates into a foreach call behind the scenes:

```
def pad2(width: Int) = {
  for (_ <- 1 to width - sb.length) { sb += '*' }
  sb
}
```

Even better, you can use the existing padTo method on StringBuilder:

```
scala> println(new StringBuilder("Hello, kitteh!")
          .padTo(20, '*').mkString)
Hello, kitteh!******
```

```
scala> println(new StringBuilder("U go now.")
         .padTo(20, '*').mkString)
U go now.***********
```

 Watch out when passing expressions to
foreach that return a function. More
generally, before writing your own utility
code, check if a suitable method already exists
in the Scala collections library.

Puzzler 22

Cast Away

Although all values in Scala are objects, its basic value types (Byte, Short, Int, *etc.*) are compiled where possible into their primitive counterparts in Java. This allows you to think of instances of those types as regular objects, simplifying the programming model. Treating Java primitives as Scala value types also makes working with Java libraries easier.

By contrast, no similar translation exists between Java and Scala collection types—you have to convert between them. Scala provides two objects, JavaConversions and JavaConverters, to help you deal with such conversions. JavaConverters is usually preferred, because it makes the conversions more obvious in the code.

The following program showcases the use of a Java collection in Scala. What does it do?

```scala
import collection.JavaConverters._

def javaMap: java.util.Map[String, java.lang.Integer] = {
  val map =
    new java.util.HashMap[String, java.lang.Integer]()
  map.put("key", null)
  map
}

val scalaMap = javaMap.asScala
val scalaTypesMap =
  scalaMap.asInstanceOf[scala.collection.Map[String, Int]]

println(scalaTypesMap("key") == null)
println(scalaTypesMap("key") == 0)
```

125

Possibilities

1. Prints:

   ```
   true
   true
   ```

2. Both `println` statements throw a `NullPointerException`.

3. Prints:

   ```
   true
   false
   ```

4. Prints:

   ```
   false
   true
   ```

Explanation

As a first step, let's walk through the program. As its name implies, the `javaMap` method mimics calling into a Java library. It returns a Java map with Java key and value types.

   The `asScala` method converts the Java map to a Scala map:

```
scala> javaMap
res0: java.util.Map[String,Integer] = {key=null}

scala> val scalaMap = javaMap.asScala
scalaMap: scala.collection.mutable.Map[String,Integer] =
  Map(key -> null)
```

At this point, you have a Scala map, but the value type `java.lang.Integer` looks a bit unusual to a Scala programmer's eye. In order to switch to Scala types, you can cast the `java.lang.Integer` to `scala.Int`:

126

```
scala> val scalaTypesMap = scalaMap.asInstanceOf[
         scala.collection.Map[String, Int]]
scalaTypesMap: scala.collection.Map[String,Int] =
  Map(key -> null)
```

Having finally arrived at a native Scala map, you can start using it—in this case, in the two subsequent `println` statements.

You may have noticed that the result of the last code snippet revealed that the actual value of `scalaTypesMap` was `Map(key -> null)`. You might therefore assume that the first `println` statement must produce `true` and the second `false` (*i.e.*, candidate answer number 3).

The REPL tells a different story:

```
scala> println(scalaTypesMap("key") == null)
true

scala> println(scalaTypesMap("key") == 0)
true
```

So the correct answer is number 1. How is it possible for a value to be equal to `null` and 0 at the same time? In essence, the problem lies in the casting of `scalaMap` and the fact that `java.lang.Integer` and `scala.Int` are unfortunately not *quite* the same.

You may have noticed that `scalaTypesMap` contains the value `null` even though the type of its values is `Int`. Values of type `Int` should by definition never be `null`, since `Int` extends `AnyVal`.[1] Here, however, `null` is *inside a collection*. This is important, because Scala collections, like Java collections (except for arrays), cannot store Java primitive types directly. Because collections are generic, and generic classes are subject to type erasure, the type of collection elements is erased to `AnyRef` (`java.lang.Object`). All Scala's value types, including `Int`, are `AnyVal`s and thus need to be *boxed* into `AnyRef` wrapper types when stored in a collection.[2] So every Scala `Map[String, Int]` actually contains `Integer` values under the covers. Reading `Integer` values out of a `Map[String, Int]` is thus what the compiler does all the time.

The real action of the puzzler lies in the two `println` statements. The first `println` statement compares the map value to `null`:

---

[1] See Puzzler 28 for a more detailed discussion of value types.
[2] Odersky, Spoon, Venners, *Programming in Scala*, [Ode10]

```
println(scalaTypesMap("key") == null)
```

Because the value extracted from the map is an AnyRef wrapper type, it is compared to null (also an AnyRef) directly. The unsurprising result of null == null is true.

The second println statement, on the other hand, compares the map value with zero:

```
println(scalaTypesMap("key") == 0)
```

For performance reasons, the compiler will always try to carry out operations on primitive types where possible, instead of on wrapper types. This means that the compiler *unboxes* the wrapper type extracted from the map, which results in code similar to:

```
println(unbox(scalaTypesMap("key")) == 0)
```

If you decompile the code example, you can see the exact calls the compiler uses to perform the unboxing:

```
Predef$.MODULE$.println(BoxesRunTime.boxToBoolean(
  scalaTypesMap.apply("key") == null));
Predef$.MODULE$.println(BoxesRunTime.boxToBoolean(
  BoxesRunTime.unboxToInt(scalaTypesMap.apply("key")) == 0));
```

Method BoxesRunTime.unboxToInt is implemented as follows:[3]

```
public static int unboxToInt(Object i) {
  return i == null ? 0 : ((java.lang.Integer)i).intValue();
}
```

This is why when the result of scalaTypesMap("key") is unboxed for the second println statement, zero is returned. As a result, this equality comparison *also* evaluates to true.

You can observe the behavior just described by examining the output of certain compiler phases. The most relevant one here is the *erasure* phase. Passing the –Xprint:erasure option to the compiler prints the following (simplified for clarity):

---

[3]The BoxesRunTime.unboxToInt logic differs from that of Predef.Integer2int and scala.Int.unbox, which when passed null throw a NullPointerException.

```
def javaMap(): java.util.Map = {
  val map: java.util.HashMap = new java.util.HashMap();
  map.put("key", null);
  map
};
// types erased
val scalaMap: collection.mutable.Map =
  mapAsScalaMapConverter(javaMap()).asScala()
  .asInstanceOf[collection.mutable.Map]();
val scalaTypesMap: collection.Map =
  scalaMap.asInstanceOf[collection.Map]();
println(scala.Boolean.box(
  scalaTypesMap.apply("key").==(null)));
// wrapper type unboxed to primitive
println(scala.Boolean.box(
  unbox(scalaTypesMap.apply("key")).==(0)))
```

Discussion

You might be wondering what would happen if you tried the same set of println statements against scalaMap, which retains the original Java key and value types:

```
println(scalaMap("key") == null)
println(scalaMap("key") == 0)
```

Notice the difference after the erasure phase:

```
println(scala.Boolean.box(scalaMap.apply("key").==(null)));
println(scala.Boolean.box(
  scalaMap.apply("key").==(scala.Int.box(0))))
```

The crucial difference is in the last statement. Instead of unboxing the map value, which has type `java.lang.Integer`, the compiler boxes the literal zero and compares the resulting AnyRefs. This time the result is more in line with expectations:

```
scala> println(scalaMap("key") == null)
true

scala> println(scalaMap("key") == 0)
false
```

In short, a wrapped value type stored in a collection will be unboxed when compared against another value type. If the declared type of the collection is a wrapper type, by contrast, no unboxing will occur and the the value type will be boxed instead.

Casts are inherently unsafe and should be generally avoided, because they bypass type checking entirely. In particular, casting Scala value to Java wrapper types, and *vice versa*, can produce unexpected results. Let the compiler handle the conversions implicitly instead of explicitly casting yourself.

Puzzler 23

Adaptive Reasoning

Scala supports two ways of passing arguments:

1. *By-value*, which causes arguments to be evaluated before being passed to the method. This is the default.

2. *By-name*, which causes arguments to be evaluated only when referenced inside the method.[1] By-name parameters are prefixed with the => symbol.

By-name parameters are useful in situations where you want to avoid evaluating an argument before a method call, especially if the evaluation is expensive. However, unlike lazy values, by-name parameters are evaluated *each time* they are referenced inside a method:

```
def mod(a: => Double) = if (a >= 0) a else -a
scala> mod({ println("evaluating"); -5.2 })
evaluating
evaluating
res0: Double = 5.2
```

Another nice feature of Scala is that it allows you to omit parentheses when passing a block. This can give method calls the look and feel of a built-in control structure[2]:

```
List(1, 2, 3) foreach { e => println(math.abs(e)) }
```

---

[1]Odersky, *The Scala Language Specification*, Section 4.6.1. [Ode14]

[2]Curly braces and parentheses in method calls also feature in Puzzler 35.

131

The following program combines both of these features. What does it do?

```scala
class Printer(prompter: => Unit) {
  def print(message: String, prompted: Boolean = false) {
    if (prompted) prompter
    println(message)
  }
}

def prompt() {
  print("puzzler$ ")
}

new Printer { prompt } print (message = "Puzzled yet?")
new Printer { prompt } print (message = "Puzzled yet?",
  prompted = true)
```

Possibilities

1. Prints:

   ```
   Puzzled yet?
   puzzler$ Puzzled yet?
   ```

2. Prints:

   ```
   puzzler$ Puzzled yet?
   puzzler$ Puzzled yet?
   ```

3. Prints:

   ```
   puzzler$ Puzzled yet?
   Puzzled yet?
   ```

4. Fails to compile.

Explanation

The two invocations of `Printer.print` seem to follow the same code path:

1. A new instance of `Printer` is created, with method `prompt` passed as the constructor argument, `prompter`.

2. Parameter `prompter` is by-name, so it is not evaluated yet and nothing is printed to the console.

3. Method `print` is invoked. In the first invocation, no value is provided for `prompter` so it takes the specified default value, `false`. Thus, `prompter` is never invoked and only the value of `message` is printed. The second call to `print`, with `prompted` explicitly set to `true`, causes `prompter` to be invoked before `message` is output.

So the first candidate answer seems to be correct. Unfortunately, when you run the code you'll find the REPL does not agree. The correct answer is number 2!

```
scala> new Printer { prompt } print (message =
          "Puzzled yet?")
puzzler$ Puzzled yet?

scala> new Printer { prompt } print (message =
          "Puzzled yet?", prompted = true)
puzzler$ Puzzled yet?
```

The fact that the output is the same for both invocations of `print` is rather interesting. It turns out the above analysis missed something crucial related to the way in which constructor arguments are passed. Specifically, curly braces can be used in place of parentheses only in the case of *method* arguments. Constructor arguments, on the other hand, always need to be provided within parentheses.

In short, the following expressions are *not* equivalent:

```
new Printer(prompt)
new Printer { prompt }
```

The former creates a new instance of `Printer` with `prompt` as the constructor argument. The latter does something very different: it instantiates an anonymous subclass with a no-arg, primary constructor. So, instead of prompt being passed as a constructor argument, it ends up being invoked as part of the constructor of the anonymous subclass.

Nonetheless, Printer *has* a class parameter (prompter) and it does not look as if a value is being provided when creating the new instances. If prompt is *not* being passed as a constructor argument, how does the code even compile, seeing as Printer declares a class parameter?

The first step of the explanation can be found in *The Scala Language Specification*, which specifies that if no explicit constructor arguments are given, an empty argument list, (), is supplied.[3] So the first call to print actually looks like this:

```scala
new Printer() { prompt } print (message = "Puzzled yet?")
```

But this also does not provide a constructor argument, so it is still not clear how the code compiles. This is where another language feature, *argument adaptation*, comes into play: the compiler attempts to "fix" missing arguments in an argument list by adding the Unit value, (), and seeing if the result type checks.[4] This yields the following expression:

```scala
new Printer(()) { prompt } print (message = "Puzzled yet?")
```

Now you finally see all of the pieces of the puzzle. Since method prompt is part of the class definition (the no-arg primary constructor, to be more precise) it is executed in both cases, as soon as Printer is instantiated. When invoked, the Unit value, (), which is passed as the value of prompter, does nothing. Hence, both calls to print result in identical output.

Discussion

Running this in a REPL with the –Xlint option results in a warning:[5]

```scala
scala> new Printer { prompt } print (message =
          "Puzzled yet?")
<console>:10: warning: Adapting argument list
   by inserting (): this is unlikely to be what you want.
```

---

[3] Odersky, *The Scala Language Specification*, Section 5.1.1. [Ode14]
[4] See Puzzler 32 for a more detailed discussion of argument adaptation.
[5] This warning is given by default in Scala 2.11, which deprecates argument adaptation.

134

```
        signature: Printer(prompter: => Unit): Printer
  given arguments: <none>
 after adaptation: new Printer((): Unit)
    new Printer { prompt } print (message = "Puzzled yet?")
         ^

puzzler$ Puzzled yet?
```

To achieve the intended behavior, all you have to do is use parentheses to ensure `prompt` is passed as a constructor argument:

```
scala> new Printer(prompt) print (message = "Puzzled yet?")
Puzzled yet?
```

```
scala> new Printer(prompt) print (message = "Puzzled yet?",
           prompted = true)
puzzler$ Puzzled yet?
```

Remember that you always need to enclose constructor arguments in parentheses. You can replace parentheses with curly braces only when specifying method arguments.

Puzzler 24

Double Trouble

One of the differences between floating-point and integer arithmetic is the
existence of the special floating-point value NaN. By and large, this value
behaves predictably, but you still need to bear in mind how it can affect
affect your code.

This code example sorts two collections of floating-point values. What
is the result of executing the following code?

```
def printSorted(a: Array[Double]) {
  util.Sorting.stableSort(a)
  println(a.mkString(" "))
}
printSorted(Array(7.89, Double.NaN, 1.23, 4.56))
printSorted(Array(7.89, 1.23, Double.NaN, 4.56))
```

Possibilities

1. Prints:

    ```
    1.23 4.56 7.89 NaN
    1.23 4.56 7.89 NaN
    ```

2. Prints:

    ```
    1.23 4.56 7.89 NaN
    1.23 7.89 NaN 4.56
    ```

137

3. Prints:

```
NaN 1.23 4.56 7.89
NaN 1.23 4.56 7.89
```

4. Prints:

```
1.23 4.56 7.89 NaN
1.23 4.56 NaN 7.89
```

Explanation

You may ask yourself whether `Double.NaN` is regarded as greater, or smaller, than all other `Double`s? Or does sorting leave NaNs in place? Surely, though, the presence of NaN values cannot cause arrays to be incorrectly sorted?

Oh, yes, it can—sometimes. The correct answer is number 2:

```
scala> printSorted(Array(7.89, Double.NaN, 1.23, 4.56))
1.23 4.56 7.89 NaN

scala> printSorted(Array(7.89, 1.23, Double.NaN, 4.56))
1.23 7.89 NaN 4.56
```

To understand what is going on here, you first need to consider a few of the properties of NaN. To adhere to IEEE 754,[1] comparisons involving NaN using ==, <, >, <=, and >= always result in `false` in Java and Scala. Comparisons involving NaN using != always result in `true`.

```
scala> 1.0 < Double.NaN
res0: Boolean = false

scala> 1.0 > Double.NaN
res1: Boolean = false

scala> Double.NaN != Double.NaN
res2: Boolean = true
```

---

[1] IEEE 754 is the Standard for Floating-Point Arithmetic.

As of 2.10.0,[2] Scala's default implicit `Ordering` for `Double`, which is used by `util.Sorting`, adheres to IEEE 754. As a result, *Ordering on Double is inconsistent*. For example, `compare(1.0, Double.NaN)` is negative, implying that `1.0` is less than `Double.NaN`. On the other hand, the direct comparison `lt(1.0, Double.NaN)` returns `false`, in accordance with the IEEE criteria. This implies that `1.0` is *not* less than `Double.NaN`:

```
val doubleOps = implicitly[Ordering[Double]]

scala> doubleOps.compare(1.0, Double.NaN)
res12: Int = -1

scala> doubleOps.lt(1.0, Double.NaN)
res13: Boolean = false
```

This inconsistency is the fundamental reason for the observed behavior of the code example. To see how this causes the second array in the code example, `Array(7.89, 1.23, Double.NaN, 4.56)`, to be incorrectly sorted, you need to look more closely at the implementation of `Sorting.stableSort`, Scala's default stable sorting algorithm that is intended for almost-sorted arrays and sequences.[3]

To sort an array, `stableSort` first divides it down the middle and recursively sorts the resulting subarrays, by default using `Ordering.lt` to compare elements. To produce the final result, it then merges the two sorted subarrays by taking elements from the first subarray as long as they are less than or equal to—again according to `Ordering.lt`—the current "reference element" of the second subarray. The reference element (initially, the first element) is added to the result array only if is *greater*, whereupon the next element of the second subarray becomes the new reference.

The soundness of this process relies critically on the fact that the second subarray is assumed to be sorted: in that case, if the current element of the first half is less than or equal to the reference element of the second half, it is necessarily also less than or equal to all the *subsequent* elements in that half.

What happens in the case of the second array in the code example? First, `stableSort` recursively sorts `7.89`, `1.23`, and `Double.NaN`, `4.56`, resulting in the sorted subarrays `1.23`, `7.89`, and `Double.NaN`, `4.56`. The second subarray is indeed correctly sorted according to the IEEE specification, since `Ordering.lt(4.56, Double.NaN)` is false, *i.e.*, `Double.NaN <= 4.56`.

---

[2]See SI-5104, "(Double.NaN min 0.0) yields 0.0, should be NaN." [Dou]

[3]A sorting algorithm is *stable* if it leaves the order of equal elements unchanged.

Now, the algorithm starts the merge process, comparing the current element of the first half, 1.23, with the reference element of the second half, Double.NaN. Since 1.23 is less than or equal to Double.NaN (according to Ordering.lt), it is added to the result array. Then, stableSort compares 7.89, the next element of the first half, with Double.NaN and *again* concludes that, because it is less than or equal to Double.NaN, it should be added to the result array.

Herein lies the error: while Ordering.lt(Double.NaN, 7.89), *i.e.*, 7.89 <= Double.NaN, is true, the conclusion that 7.89 is thus less than all subsequent elements in the second subarray—4.56, in this case—is false. By this point, however, both elements from the first subarray have already been processed. The algorithm concludes that any remaining elements in the second subarray must be larger than all the values already added to the result array, so it simply adds them to the result.

Discussion

The presence of the "unusual" Double.NaN value can at least give you a hint of what might be causing the unexpected behavior. Figuring out what is going on becomes a lot more difficult if there is any kind of "data cleanup" happening that strips out such values. Imagine trying to debug the following:

```scala
import util.Sorting.stableSort
def filterNaN(arr: Array[Double]) = arr filter { !_.isNaN() }
val filterBeforeSort =
  filterNaN(Array(1.23, 7.89, Double.NaN, 4.56))
stableSort(filterBeforeSort)
scala> println(filterBeforeSort mkString " ")
1.23 4.56 7.89

val sortBeforeFilter = Array(1.23, 7.89, Double.NaN, 4.56)
stableSort(sortBeforeFilter)
scala> println(filterNaN(sortBeforeFilter) mkString " ")
1.23 7.89 4.56
```

Here, there really is *no* indication of what might be happening—you are simply getting an incorrectly sorted array.

140

To avoid this problem, define an ordering for Double—or pass an explicit comparison function to the sorting algorithms—that consistently handles NaN. Double.compare, which, like java.lang.Double.compareTo, treats Double.NaN as equal to itself and greater than all other Double values, is a useful candidate:

```
def printSortedByDoubleCompare(a: Array[Double]) {
  def ltWithNaNGtAll(x: Double, y: Double) =
    (x compare y) < 0
  util.Sorting.stableSort(a, ltWithNaNGtAll _)
  println(a.mkString(" "))
}
scala> printSortedByDoubleCompare(
    Array(7.89, Double.NaN, 1.23, 4.56))
1.23 4.56 7.89 NaN

scala> printSortedByDoubleCompare(
    Array(7.89, 1.23, Double.NaN, 4.56))
1.23 4.56 7.89 NaN
```

Note that the behavior of Double.compare is *not* IEEE 754-compliant. Surprising as it may seem, there is no way of ordering Doubles that handles NaN consistently and is compliant with the IEEE specification.

As of Scala 2.10.0, sorting Doubles using the default orderings does not correctly handle NaN. Define your own orderings, or provide explicit comparison functions to sorting algorithms when sorting collections of Doubles that may contain NaN.

Puzzler 25

Type Extortion

Many methods in the Scala collections library have a return type of Option, indicating they may fail to deliver a value. The recommended way to extract the value out of an Option is via the getOrElse method, which allows you to provide a default value in case the Option is empty.

The following program shows an example of getOrElse in action. What does it do?

```
val zippedLists = (List(1,3,5), List(2,4,6)).zipped
val (x, y) = zippedLists.find(_._1 > 10).getOrElse(10)

println(s"Found $x")
```

Possibilities

1. Prints:

   Found 10

2. Prints:

   Found ()

3. Fails to compile.

4. Throws a runtime exception.

Explanation

Before trying to understand what is going on here, it is useful to quickly recap the behavior of zipped via a short example:

```
scala> val zippedLists = (List(1,3,5), List(2,4,6)).zipped
zippedLists: scala.runtime.Tuple2Zipped[Int,List[Int],
  Int,List[Int]] = scala.runtime.Tuple2Zipped@3d38da0d

scala> zippedLists.toList // force evaluation
res0: List[(Int, Int)] = List((1,2), (3,4), (5,6))
```

In short, zipped takes matching elements of the two lists, combines them into tuples, and returns a sequence of such tuples as its result.

Now that you are sure what zipped does, you can go back to the puzzler. Method find searches for the first tuple that matches a predicate, in this case, a tuple whose first element is greater than 10. If find returns None, the default value provided to the getOrElse method will be returned. Note that Int, the type of the default value, does not match (Int, Int), the type of the elements find is examining. Since the result of the expression has to be assigned to a tuple of two elements, the code will fail to compile, right? In other words, the third candidate answer must be correct.

Let's check:

```
scala> val zippedLists = (List(1,3,5), List(2,4,6)).zipped
zippedLists: scala.runtime.Tuple2Zipped[Int,List[Int],
  Int,List[Int]] = scala.runtime.Tuple2Zipped@3d38da0d

scala> val (x, y) = zippedLists.find(_._1 > 10).getOrElse(10)
scala.MatchError: 10 (of class java.lang.Integer)
```

Rather than failing to compile, the code throws an exception at runtime! The correct answer is actually number 4.

What was missed is that calling getOrElse on an instance of Option[A] does not necessarily return a value of type A:

```
final def getOrElse[B >: A](default: => B): B
```

Option.getOrElse is not the only method with such *widening* behavior. Methods such as Option.orElse, Try.recover, and Future.recover can also return a wider type than the original element type.

In the code example, the inferred return type is Any—the most specific supertype of Tuple2 and Int:

```scala
scala> zippedLists.find(_._1 > 10).getOrElse(10)
res0: Any = 10
```

Why does the compiler not complain about a type mismatch? After all, a value of type Any cannot be assigned to a val of type Tuple2. But that is not what is actually happening in the code example. There, the tuple instead represents a *pattern definition:*[1,2]

```scala
val (x, y) = zippedLists.find(_._1 > 10).getOrElse(10)
```

This expands into the following expression:

```scala
val a$ = zippedLists.find(_._1 > 10).getOrElse(10) match {
  case (b, c) => (b, c)
}
val x = a$._1
val y = a$._2
```

In other words, the code example compiles without problems but throws an exception at runtime when the pattern match fails.

Tuple vals and tuple patterns

Note the subtle syntactic difference between the definition of a val of a tuple type and one involving a tuple pattern:

```scala
val tup: (Int, Int) = ...      // regular
val (x: Int, y: Int) = ...     // pattern
```

---

[1] Odersky, *The Scala Language Specification*, Section 4.1. [Ode14]
[2] See Puzzler 2 for a detailed discussion of pattern definitions.

Discussion

To prevent the compiler from inferring wider types than intended, you can explicitly stipulate the desired type:

```
scala> val (x, y): (Int, Int) =
          zippedLists.find(_._1 > 10).getOrElse(10)
<console>:9: error: type mismatch;
 found    : Int(10)
 required: (Int, Int)
        val (x, y): (Int, Int) =
          zippedLists.find(_._1 > 10).getOrElse(10)
                                                 ^
```

It is possible to run into problems with widening in circumstances where the type mismatch would be less evident. As an example, consider the following code snippet, where the incorrect order of Int and String goes unnoticed:

```
def howToPronounce(numAndName: Option[(Int, String)]) = {
  val (num, name) = numAndName.getOrElse(("eight", 8))
  println(s"The word for $num is '$name'")
}
scala> howToPronounce(Some((7, "seven")))
The word for 7 is 'seven'

scala> howToPronounce(None)
The word for eight is '8'
```

This is not what you would expect. The compiler infers (Any, Any) as the return type of getOrElse, so both num and name end up with type Any. To avoid such surprises at runtime, make sure you also test the code path that uses the fallback value.

Be aware that many methods that allow for a fallback value can return a *wider* type than intended. In view of that, specify the expected return type for any non-trivial expressions involving these methods.

Puzzler 26

Accepts Any Args

Scala supports both multiple-parameter and multiple-parameter *list* (*i.e.*, curried) definitions of functions. This gives you quite a bit of freedom when defining functions, but also means that some rework can be required if you decide to change a function's "parameter style."

In the following example, a method that starts out with a single parameter list with two parameters is refactored to use curried parameters. Both forms of the method are then invoked, unchanged, before and after refactoring.

What is the result of executing the following code?

```scala
def prependIfLong(candidate: Any, elems: Any*): Seq[Any] = {
  if (candidate.toString.length > 1)
    candidate +: elems
  else
    elems
}
println(prependIfLong("I", "love", "Scala")(0))

def prependIfLongRefac(candidate: Any)(elems: Any*):
    Seq[Any] = {
  if (candidate.toString.length > 1)
    candidate +: elems
  else
    elems
}
// invoked unchanged
println(prependIfLongRefac("I", "love", "Scala")(0))
```

147

Possibilities

1. Prints:

   ```
   love
   love
   ```

2. Prints:

   ```
   love
   ArrayBuffer((I,love,Scala), 0)
   ```

3. Prints:

   ```
   love
   IloveScala
   ```

4. The first `println` statement prints:

   ```
   love
   ```

   and the second fails to compile.

Explanation

You may wonder whether the compiler can apply some kind of "compatibility transformation" to adapt the unchanged invocation to the new curried declaration. If not, the second `prependIfLongRefac` invocation must surely fail to compile?

Not quite:

```
scala> println(prependIfLong("I", "love", "Scala")(0))
love

scala> println(prependIfLongRefac("I", "love", "Scala")(0))
ArrayBuffer((I,love,Scala), 0)
```

The correct answer, therefore, is number 2. Let's first briefly step through the "pre-refactoring" invocation, which behaves as expected. Here, the first argument, "I", is bound to prependIfLong's candidate parameter, and "love" and "Scala" are bound to the second vararg parameter, elems. "I" is not longer than one character, so prependIfLong returns the vararg sequence WrappedArray("love", "Scala") unchanged. Its first element "love" is then printed:

```
val prepended = prependIfLong("I", "love", "Scala")

scala> println(prepended(0))
love
```

So far, so straightforward. The second invocation, after the refactoring, is where things get interesting. The most surprising fact is perhaps that the *unchanged* invocation still compiles successfully. The println statement produces a rather unexpected output, though: you certainly no longer appear to be printing the first element of the returned sequence.

How does the compiler manage to compile this call? After refactoring, prependIfLongRefac expects an initial argument list with a *single* argument. Yet *three* arguments are still being passed, matching the original multi-parameter declaration of prependIfLong!

Here, a feature not documented in the language specification comes into play. After the compiler has unsuccessfully attempted to find a version of prependIfLongRefac that can take three arguments, it tries one last option: packing all arguments into a tuple and trying to apply the function to that. This *auto-tupling* actually succeeds in this case, binding candidate to the three-tuple, ("I", "love", "Scala").

At this point, all the arguments intended for prependIfLongRefac have been exhausted, so what about the second vararg parameter, elems? Here, the compiler simply "grabs" the (0) application that is supposed to extract the first element from the method result! It therefore ends up printing the *entire* result consisting (since candidate.toString is certainly longer than one character) of candidate prepended to elems.

In other words, the second invocation is equivalent to:

```
val prepended = prependIfLongRefac(("I", "love", "Scala"))(0)

scala> println(prepended)
ArrayBuffer((I,love,Scala), 0)
```

149

Discussion

You can use the -Ywarn-adapted-args and -Yno-adapted-args compiler flags to warn and fail, respectively, on occurrences of auto-tupling:[1]

-Ywarn-adapted-args Warn if an argument list is modified to match the receiver.

```
scala> :settings +Ywarn-adapted-args

scala> println(prependIfLongRefac("I", "love", "Scala") _)
<console>:9: warning: Adapting argument list by creating
  a 3-tuple: this may not be what you want.
        signature: prependIfLongRefac(candidate: Any)
          (elems: Any*): Seq[Any]
    given arguments: "I", "love", "Scala"
   after adaptation: prependIfLongRefac(("I", "love", "Scala"):
    (String, String, String))
              println(prependIfLongRefac(
                                         ^

<function1>
```

-Yno-adapted-args Do not adapt an argument list to match the receiver.

```
scala> :settings +Yno-adapted-args

scala> println(prependIfLongRefac("I", "love", "Scala") _)
<console>:9: error: too many arguments for method
  prependIfLongRefac: (candidate: Any)(elems: Any*)Seq[Any]
            println(prependIfLongRefac(
                                       ^
```

Specifying the first argument as a *named* argument is another way to prevent the compiler from silently auto-tupling:

```
scala> println(prependIfLong(
          candidate = "I", "love", "Scala")(0))
love
```

---

[1]Unfortunately, the warnings and failures are not triggered if the adaptation does not occur in the *last* argument list.

```
scala> println(prependIfLongRefac(
         candidate = "I", "love", "Scala")(0))
<console>:9: error: too many arguments for method
  prependIfLongRefac: (candidate: Any)(elems: Any*)Seq[Any]
              println(prependIfLongRefac(
                               ^
```

 When defining methods or functions with
parameters of type Any, and especially when
refactoring such methods, be aware of the
possibility of auto-tupling. If desired, use the
compiler flags -Ywarn-adapted-args and
-Yno-adapted-args to warn of or prevent
auto-tupling.

Puzzler 27

A Case of Strings

One of Scala's strengths is its interoperability with Java, which allows you to reuse Java libraries and tools without performance penalties. From Scala you can access and extend Java classes, call Java methods, *etc.*

Unfortunately, Java methods often return null, usually to indicate that no data is available. Although this is a common Java idiom, the ambiguous nature of null causes problems. It is frequently unclear whether the return value of null represents uninitialized, non-existent, or empty values. Besides, it might not be obvious to the caller of a method that null is a possible return value, and as a result, they may forget to explicitly check for null. This causes an astounding number of bugs.

The following program illustrates one such case, where null is returned from a Java method. For conciseness, invoking a Java method is simulated by returning null explicitly—no actual Java method is invoked. What does the program do?

```scala
def objFromJava: Object = "string"
def stringFromJava: String = null

def printLengthIfString(a: AnyRef): Unit = a match {
  case str: String =>
      println(s"String of length ${str.length}")
  case _ => println("Not a string")
}

printLengthIfString(objFromJava)
printLengthIfString(stringFromJava)
```

Possibilities

1. Prints:

   ```
   Not a string
   String of length 0
   ```

2. The first call to `printLengthIfString` prints:

   ```
   Not a string
   ```

   and the second throws a `NullPointerException`.

3. Prints:

   ```
   String of length 6
   Not a string
   ```

4. The first call to `printLengthIfString` prints:

   ```
   String of length 6
   ```

   and the second throws a `NullPointerException`.

Explanation

The correct answer is number 3:

```
scala> printLengthIfString(objFromJava)
String of length 6

scala> printLengthIfString(stringFromJava)
Not a string
```

To understand why, it helps to look at the literal `null` from Scala's point of view. Consider the Scala class hierarchy, shown in Figure 27.1.

Notice `Null` at the bottom of the hierarchy, just above `Nothing`. `Null` is a special type included in Scala solely for compatibility with Java. It has exactly one instance: `null`. The type `Null` is a subtype of all reference

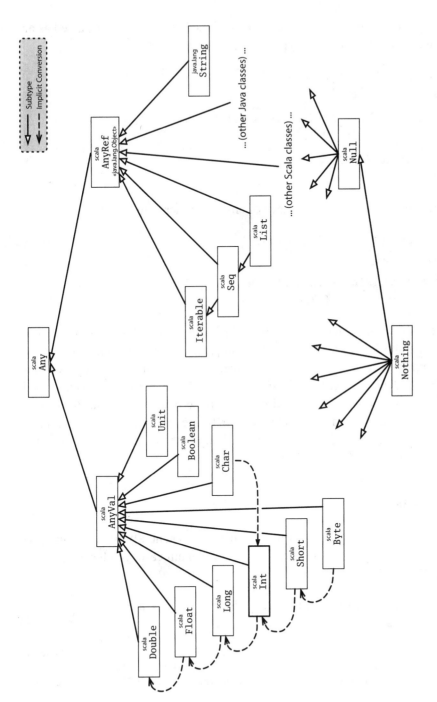

Figure 27.1 · Class hierarchy of Scala.

155

types, and consequently, null can be assigned to a variable or passed as an argument of any reference type:

```scala
scala> val s: String = null
s: String = null

scala> def say(s: String) = println(s)
say: (s: String)Unit

scala> say(null)
null
```

However, null is not an instance of any type other than Null:

```scala
scala> val s: String = null
s: String = null

scala> s.isInstanceOf[String]
res0: Boolean = false
```

The reason this behavior, which Scala inherits from Java,[1] is relevant is because the key part of our code example is the pattern matching in the printLengthIfString method. In Scala, pattern matching on types is implemented via the isInstanceOf method, which performs checks based on runtime type. So, it should be no surprise that the first call to method printLengthIfString matches the first case statement, and the second falls through to the default case, even though the compile-time type of the value stringFromJava is String.

Discussion

If you pattern match against a value that can potentially be null and you want the matching to handle null as a non-default case, you have to explicitly check for a null value:

```scala
def printLengthIfString(a: AnyRef): Unit = a match {
  case null => println("Got null!")
```

---

[1] From *Java Language Specification*, Version 7, Section 15.20.2: At run time, the result of the instanceOf operator is true if the value of the *RelationalExpression* is not null and the reference could be cast to the *ReferenceType* without raising a ClassCastException. Otherwise the result is false.

```scala
    case str: String =>
        println(s"String of length ${str.length}")
    case _ => println("Not a string")
}
```

On the other hand, it is good practice in Scala to take advantage of the Option factory, which returns None if the argument is null:

```scala
scala> def objFromJava: Object = "string"
objFromJava: Object

scala> def stringFromJava: String = null
stringFromJava: String

scala> Option(objFromJava)
res0: Option[Object] = Some(string)

scala> Option(stringFromJava)
res1: Option[String] = None
```

Option allows you to check for None where you would have checked for null, transforming NullPointerExceptions into compiler errors. Using Options also allows you to chain computations involving optional values in for expressions instead of testing for null in nested if-else clauses.

Bear in mind that typed patterns in Scala match against runtime, not compile-time types. As a result, they will not match null as that is not an instance of any type other than Null. Add an explicit match against the null value to act on null, or preferably, wrap the result of any method call that may return null in an Option and check for None instead.

Puzzler 28

Pick a Value, AnyValue!

Scala's abstract type members allow you to define base classes without immediately committing to specific implementation types. You could, for instance, define a `Recipe` without having to decide up front how precise you need the amounts to be, *i.e.*, which numeric type to use for quantities:

```scala
trait Recipe {
  type T <: AnyVal
  def sugarAmount: T
  def howMuchSugar() {
    println(s"Add ${sugarAmount} tablespoons of sugar")
  }
}
val approximateCake = new Recipe {
  type T = Int
  val sugarAmount = 5
}
scala> approximateCake.howMuchSugar()
Add 5 tablespoons of sugar

val gourmetCake = new Recipe {
  type T = Double
  val sugarAmount = 5.13124
}
scala> gourmetCake.howMuchSugar()
Add 5.13124 tablespoons of sugar
```

159

If you want to initialize a variable of the abstract type in the base class, you cannot in general use a specific value, since the type itself is not yet known. You *can*, however, initialize a var to the default value for its type by setting it to _ (*i.e.*, underscore).[1]

What is the result of executing the following code in the REPL?

```scala
trait NutritionalInfo {
  type T <: AnyVal
  var value: T = _
}
val containsSugar = new NutritionalInfo { type T = Boolean }
println(containsSugar.value)
println(!containsSugar.value)
```

Possibilities

1. Prints:

   ```
   false
   true
   ```

2. Prints:

   ```
   false
   false
   ```

3. The first statement prints:

   ```
   null
   ```

   and the second throws an exception.

4. Prints:

   ```
   null
   true
   ```

---

[1] Odersky, *The Scala Language Specification*, Section 4.2. [Ode14]

Explanation

You may wonder whether the value of `Booleans` initialized to their default by setting them to _ is, for some reason, *not* false. Or you may suspect that the variable starts out as `null` despite being a `Boolean`, and throws a `NullPointerException` when you try to negate.

In fact, this is almost the case—but not quite. The correct answer is number 4:

```
scala> println(containsSugar.value)
null

scala> println(!containsSugar.value)
true
```

How can a `Boolean` value be `null`? After all, the compiler "knows" at the moment of initialization that the variable will be an `AnyVal`. Even if the compiler internally uses `null`, for whatever reason, why is this visible to the program? And why do you then not see a `NullPointerException` when you try to negate the value?

Surprising as it may seem, the fact that your `AnyVal` variable is initialized to `null` is not a compiler trick of some kind. It is stated explicitly in the language specification:[2]

> The default value depends on the type T as follows:
>
> - 0 if T is `Int` or one of its subrange types
>
> - 0L if T is `Long`
>
> - 0.0f if T is `Float`
>
> - 0.0d if T is `Double`
>
> - false if T is `Boolean`
>
> - () if T is `Unit`
>
> - null for all other types T

---

[2]Odersky, *The Scala Language Specification*, Section 4.2. [Ode14]

Even though the compiler knows at the point of initialization that your variable will be some subtype of AnyVal, it does not know *which* type. According to the language specification, null is indeed the appropriate default value in that case.

By the time you attempt to negate the value, the compiler knows, of course, that it is a Boolean. Indeed, you *have* to treat it as a Boolean in order to be able to invoke the unary_! method (Scala's boolean negation) on it. This method is defined on scala.Boolean, not inherited from any of Boolean's supertypes.

When calling unary_!, the compiler handles the task of treating the underlying java.lang.Object (with value null) as a Boolean by automatically *unboxing* it using scala.runtime.BoxesRunTime.unboxToBoolean. This method handles an underlying value of null by returning false, the default value for Booleans in Scala. Negating that value then prints "true". So far, so unspectacular.

What about the first println statement, though? At that point, the compiler *also* knows that the value is a Boolean. Why then do you see null, rather than the expected Boolean default value false?

It turns out that the cause here is the type of the argument expected by println, which is Any. When the compiler encounters the expression, println(containsSugar.value), it checks whether an instance of type java.lang.Object (the type of containsSugar.value) can be passed to println. Since println only expects an Any, this works just fine. There is no need to treat the value as a Boolean in this case, so *no unboxing is applied* and the underlying null value is printed.

Discussion

Surprisingly, this is also the case if you force the value to be treated as an AnyVal. Only if you cause it to be treated as a *Boolean* is unboxing applied:

```
def printAnyVal(a: AnyVal) { println(a) }

scala> printAnyVal(containsSugar.value)
null

def printBoolean(b: Boolean) { println(b) }

scala> printBoolean(containsSugar.value)
false
```

The compiler's refusal to unbox if the value can be treated as an Any can cause surprising NullPointerExceptions when invoking methods inherited from java.lang.Object:

```
scala> containsSugar.value equals false
java.lang.NullPointerException
  ...

scala> containsSugar.value.hashCode
java.lang.NullPointerException
  ...

scala> containsSugar.value.toString
java.lang.NullPointerException
  ...
```

Instead of equals and hashCode, you can use Scala's null-safe versions:

```
scala> containsSugar.value == false
res11: Boolean = true

scala> containsSugar.value.##
res12: Int = 1237
```

In the case of ==, the unboxing of containsSugar.value is triggered by the presence of a ==(x: Boolean) method on class Boolean, which is more specific[3] than the ==(arg0: Any) variant that Boolean inherits from Any. This forces the compiler to treat your value as a Boolean.[4]

If you really wanted to, you could force the compiler to unbox your value by using a type ascription:

```
scala> (containsSugar.value: Boolean) equals false
res13: Boolean = true

scala> (containsSugar.value: Boolean).hashCode
res14: Int = 1237
```

Note that this is not a cast, so there is no loss of type safety.

---

[3]Odersky, *The Scala Language Specification*, Section 6.26.3. [Ode14]
[4]See Puzzler 22 for a more detailed discussion of unboxing.

A more rigorous solution is to avoid initializing the variable until the specific AnyVal subtype is known. This allows the compiler to choose the appropriate default value:

```
trait NutritionalInfoNoDefault {
  type T <: AnyVal
  var value: T
}
val containsSugar2 = new NutritionalInfoNoDefault {
  type T = Boolean
  var value: T = _
}
scala> containsSugar2.value equals false
res15: Boolean = true

scala> containsSugar2.value = true
containsSugar2.value: containsSugar2.T = true
```

1. Avoid using _ to initialize variables of abstract types to their default values if those types can later be fixed to subtypes of AnyVal.

2. If you cannot avoid this, be aware that such variables may be null wherever the compiler does not need to unbox them to their declared type. Prefer Scala's null-safe == and ## methods over equals and hashCode and force unboxing before calling toString.

Puzzler 29

Implicit Kryptonite

Scala's implicits provide a flexible mechanism to access context-specific values and behavior. By changing the implicits in scope, you can switch contexts in different parts of your application easily.

This code example models a simple baggage scanner that operates in two modes, or contexts: normal operation and a special "test mode." In normal operation, the scanner's console indicates which type of item is being scanned and the alarm button is "live," triggering the alarm when activated.

To ensure that the operator keeps paying attention, the scanner also has a test mode that is activated at random intervals. In test mode, the console ignores the actual item inside the scanner and pretends to have found a dangerous item. If the operator hits the alarm button, as they should, the scanner congratulates them for completing the test successfully.

The behavior of the scanner is defined by two implicits, a console and a handler, for the two contexts, normal operation and test mode. The scanner is switched from normal to test mode as items pass through it.

What is the result of executing the following code in the REPL?

```scala
object Scanner {
  trait Console { def display(item: String) }
  trait AlarmHandler extends (() => Unit)

  def scanItem(item: String)(implicit c: Console) {
    c.display(item)
  }
  def hitAlarmButton()(implicit ah: AlarmHandler) { ah() }
}
```

```
object NormalMode {
  implicit val ConsoleRenderer = new Scanner.Console {
    def display(item: String) { println(s"Found a ${item}") }
  }
  implicit val DefaultAlarmHandler = new Scanner.AlarmHandler {
    def apply() { println("ALARM! ALARM!") }
  }
}
object TestMode {
  implicit val ConsoleRenderer = new Scanner.Console {
    def display(item: String) { println("Found a detonator") }
  }
  implicit val TestAlarmHandler = new Scanner.AlarmHandler {
    def apply() { println("Test successful. Well done!") }
  }
}
import NormalMode._
Scanner scanItem "knife"
Scanner.hitAlarmButton()

import TestMode._
Scanner scanItem "shoe"
Scanner.hitAlarmButton()
```

Possibilities

1. The first, second, and third statements print:

   ```
   Found a knife
   ALARM! ALARM!
   Found a detonator
   ```

   and the fourth fails to compile.

2. Prints:

```
Found a knife
ALARM! ALARM!
Found a detonator
Test successful. Well done!
```

3. The first and second statements print:

```
Found a knife
ALARM! ALARM!
```

and the third and fourth fail to compile.

4. Prints:

```
Found a knife
ALARM! ALARM!
Found a shoe
Test successful. Well done!
```

Explanation

You may suspect that importing the test mode implicits will cause the third and fourth statements to fail to compile due to ambiguous implicit values in scope. Otherwise, all four statements should work, or not? Surely the *names* of the implicits have no bearing on the outcome?

Actually, they do—the correct answer is number 1:

```
scala> Scanner scanItem "knife"
Found a knife

scala> Scanner.hitAlarmButton()
ALARM! ALARM!
...
scala> Scanner scanItem "shoe"
Found a detonator
```

```
scala> Scanner.hitAlarmButton()
<console>:17: error: ambiguous implicit values: both value
 DefaultAlarmHandler in object NormalMode of type
   => Scanner.AlarmHandler
 and value TestAlarmHandler in object TestMode of type
   => Scanner.AlarmHandler
 match expected type Scanner.AlarmHandler
               Scanner.hitAlarmButton()
                                      ^
```

How can this be? When the operator first hits the alarm button, the compiler is able to choose between two implicits of the same type, but not the second time around? Could this be related to the names of the implicit values? If so, isn't it the *type* of an implicit that matters, rather than the name?

Well, the type of an implicit certainly determines whether it is applicable at a particular point in the code. To understand the observed behavior, you need to look at how the compiler identifies and handles multiple applicable alternatives. And that is where the *name* of an implicit can come into play.

While you may intuitively expect implicit values to be "special" in some way, the compiler treats them like any other val or def. Therefore, when you import the test mode implicits, the `TestMode.ConsoleRenderer` shadows the previously imported `NormalMode.ConsoleRenderer`. When the compiler searches for an implicit `Console` for the second `scanItem` call, only *one* applicable implicit value is actually in scope, so the call compiles.

The two `AlarmHandler`s, however, have different names. After importing the test mode implicits, *two* applicable alternatives are therefore in scope, `NormalMode.DefaultAlarmHandler` and `TestMode.TestAlarmHandler`. The compiler then applies the standard static overloading resolution algorithm[1] to determine a most specific implicit to use—there are no "special" rules for implicits, in other words.[2] Here, neither of the two alternatives is more specific than the other, leading to the compiler error you observe.

Discussion

Obviously, you can avoid the problem by ensuring that your test mode alarm handler has the same name as the default one you intend to replace:

---

[1] Odersky, *The Scala Language Specification*, Section 6.26.3. [Ode14]
[2] Odersky, *The Scala Language Specification*, Section 7.2. [Ode14]

```scala
object TestMode2 {
  implicit val ConsoleRenderer = new Scanner.Console {
    def display(item: String) { println("Found a detonator") }
  }
  // same name as the alarm handler in NormalMode
  implicit val DefaultAlarmHandler = new Scanner.AlarmHandler {
    def apply() { println("Test successful. Well done!") }
  }
}

...

import TestMode2._

scala> Scanner scanItem "shoe"
Found a detonator

scala> Scanner.hitAlarmButton()
Test successful. Well done!
```

If you don't know the name of the implicit you are trying to "override" (*e.g.*, because you are importing it from a library), you can extract it from the "ambiguous implicit values" error message. Still, having to identify and keep track of the names of implicits you wish to override is not a particularly satisfactory solution.

Happily, Scala provides a way to override implicits *without* having to know their names. The trick is ensuring that static overload resolution regards the overriding implicits as more specific than the ones being replaced.

The standard way to do this is to define the default context in a base class or trait from which the "overriding context" inherits, as exemplified by `scala.LowPriorityImplicits`. Here, this would look something like:

```scala
...

class OperatingMode {
  implicit val ConsoleRenderer = new Scanner.Console {
    def display(item: String) { println(s"Found a ${item}") }
  }
  implicit val DefaultAlarmHandler = new Scanner.AlarmHandler {
    def apply() { println("ALARM! ALARM!") }
  }
}
```

```scala
object NormalMode extends OperatingMode

object TestMode extends OperatingMode {
  override implicit val ConsoleRenderer = new Scanner.Console {
    def display(item: String) { println("Found a detonator") }
  }
  implicit val TestAlarmHandler = new Scanner.AlarmHandler {
    def apply() { println("Test successful. Well done!") }
  }
}
```

```scala
import NormalMode._

scala> Scanner scanItem "knife"
Found a knife

scala> Scanner.hitAlarmButton()
ALARM! ALARM!

import TestMode._

scala> Scanner scanItem "shoe"
Found a detonator

scala> Scanner.hitAlarmButton()
Test successful. Well done!
```

In this version of the code example, when the compiler tries to determine the most specific applicable implicit for the second `hitAlarmButton` call, the test mode handler is more specific. To paraphrase the language specification, "`TestAlarmHandler` is defined in an object, `TestMode`, that extends the class, `OperatingMode`, defining `DefaultAlarmHandler`."[3]

Bear in mind, however, that for this approach to work the default context must explicitly be written to be extended. If the default implicits are being imported from code that you do not control, such as an external library, you have to hope that the code's authors have adhered to this pattern.

---

[3] Odersky, *The Scala Language Specification*, Section 6.26.3. [Ode14]

170

1. Names of implicits matter! Importing an implicit value of the same name and type as an existing implicit will remove the existing implicit from the set of applicable options considered by the compiler. Importing an implicit of the same type, but with a *different* name, can lead to "ambiguous implicit values" compiler errors.

2. When defining a set of implicits that are intended to be overridable, declare them in a "default context" class or trait that can be extended. Define overriding implicits in a subclass or subtrait of the default context. In this case, higher priority implicits do not need to have the same name as the implicits they are intended to replace.

Puzzler 30

Quite the Outspoken Type

Scala's powerful type inference allows you to omit type declarations in many places, leaving the compiler to figure things out. For non-trivial expressions, though, explicitly specifying types is regarded as good practice.

The following example defines two versions of an implicit conversion function from numeric strings to integers: first without, then with, an explicit type declaration. A println statement that relies on the two implicit variants follows. What is the result of executing the following code?

```scala
class QuietType {
  implicit val stringToInt = (_: String).toInt
  println("4" - 2)
}
class OutspokenType {
  implicit val stringToInt: String => Int = _.toInt
  println("4" - 2)
}
new QuietType()
new OutspokenType()
```

Possibilities

1. Prints:

   2
   2

173

2. The first statement fails to compile and the second prints:

   2

3. Both statements fail to compile.

4. The first statement prints:

   2

and the second throws a runtime exception.

Explanation

You may question whether the type inferred for `QuietType.stringToInt` and the type explicitly declared for `OutspokenType.stringToInt` are really the same, but that is indeed the case:

```
// in QuietType
scala> implicit val stringToInt = (_: String).toInt
stringToInt: String => Int = <function1>

// in OutspokenType
scala> implicit val stringToInt: String => Int = _.toInt
stringToInt: String => Int = <function1>
```

Having verified this, you may suspect instead that the implicits are not applicable to the `println` statements, resulting in compiler errors. Surely, though, explicitly specifying the return type that the compiler otherwise infers will not affect the behavior of the code?

Actually, it does—the correct answer is number 4:

```
scala> new QuietType()
2

scala> new OutspokenType()
java.lang.StackOverflowError
  at OutspokenType$$anonfun$1.apply(<console>:8)
```

A stack overflow error? How does that come about? In order to understand what happens when you construct an instance of `OutspokenType`, it is useful to start by looking at what is going on in `QuietType`.

Specifically, zoom in on the moment when the compiler has parsed the beginning of the declaration of `QuietType.stringToInt` and is trying to make sense of the expression `(_: String).toInt`. At this point, the type of `stringToInt` is as yet undetermined, since the compiler is still in the process of trying to figure it out.

Unfortunately, the compiler quickly runs up against a problem: there is, in fact, no `toInt` method on `String`. As per the language specification,[1] the compiler starts searching among all implicits in scope[2] and, conveniently, finds a suitable option: `Predef.augmentString`, which converts the string to a `StringOps` object on which `toInt` can be called.

The implicit `stringToInt` method can then be compiled successfully. It is assigned the type `String => Int` and is successfully found and applied when the subsequent `println("4" - 2)` statement is processed.

So far, so good. What, then, causes `OutspokenType` to behave so differently? Again, focus on the moment the compiler is about to process the expression `_.toInt` in the body of `OutspokenType.stringToInt`. As before, the compiler needs to invoke an implicit search, since `String` does not have a `toInt` method. The crucial difference lies here: because the type of `OutspokenType.stringToInt` is already known, it is included in the list of implicits to consider. As luck would have it, it is not only included in the list, it is even *applicable*, since `Int` also happens to have a `toInt` method.

Instead of the expected conversion to `StringOps`, what you actually end up with, therefore, is an implicit that immediately calls itself. When invoked, this results in the endless loop observed.

Discussion

An important detail not examined so far is *why* exactly the compiler chooses `stringToInt` over `augmentString` in `OutspokenType`, when both implicits are in scope. Surprisingly, it is *not* the result of static overloading resolution,[3] which is used to determine which implicit to apply. In fact, if you make a

---

[1] Odersky, *The Scala Language Specification*, Section 6.26. [Ode14]
[2] See Puzzler 29 for a more detailed discussion of implicit resolution.
[3] Odersky, *The Scala Language Specification*, Section 7.2. [Ode14]

small change and declare `stringToInt` as an implicit `def` rather than a `val`, the compiler indeed complains about ambiguous implicits:

```
scala> class OutspokenType2 {
         implicit def stringToInt(s: String): Int = s.toInt
         println("4" - 2)
       }
<console>:8: error: type mismatch;
 found    : s.type (with underlying type String)
 required: ?{def toInt: ?}
Note that implicit conversions are not applicable because
  they are ambiguous:
 both method augmentString in object Predef of type
   (x: String)scala.collection.immutable.StringOps
 and method stringToInt in class OutspokenType2 of type
   (s: String)Int
 are possible conversion functions from s.type
   to ?{def toInt: ?}
         implicit def stringToInt(s: String): Int = s.toInt
                                                        ^
```

The short answer is that function `val`s take precedence over `def`s during implicit search. The point is that this behavior is not justified by the language specification, which specifies static overloading resolution as the algorithm for determining implicit precedence. Yet overloading resolution treats "regular" `def`s and function `val`s equivalently and does not exhibit the preference for function `val`s that is observed with implicits:

```
scala> object DefAndFunVal extends App {
         def method(s: String): Int = ???
         val method: String => Int = ???
         println(method("hello"))
       }
<console>:11: error: ambiguous reference to overloaded
  definition,
 both value method in object DefAndFunVal of type
   => String => Int
 and  method method in object DefAndFunVal of type
   (s: String)Int
```

```
match argument types (String) and expected result type Any
       println(method("hello"))
                ^
```

It appears that Scala's behavior when distinguishing between def foo: T and val foo: () => T during static overloading resolution is undefined: neither the fact that the compiler treats them equivalently for explicit methods, nor that the compiler prefers the val for implicit methods, are covered by the language specification. As explained by Jason Zaugg, a member of the Scala compiler team:

> Both implicit and explicit use of static overload resolution between methods and nullary methods (*i.e.*, methods without parameters) returning function types is implementation-specific and not covered by the [language] specification.

 Prefer defs over vals when defining implicit conversions to ensure potential "ambiguous implicit" errors are not hidden by implementation-specific compiler behavior. Improve readability and safety by explicitly specifying the return type of implicit defs.

Puzzler 31

A View to a Shill

In Scala, there are often multiple ways of carrying out a given task. An example of this is transforming the elements of a map. One approach would be to use a for comprehension:

```
def translate(m: Map[String, String]): Map[String, Int] =
  for ((k, v) <- m) yield (k, v.length)
```

This is actually desugared[1] to an invocation of map with a case clause:

```
def translate(m: Map[String, String]): Map[String, Int] =
  m map { case (k, v) => (k, v.length) }
```

If only the values of a Map are being transformed, as in this example, the pattern variable k is effectively unused. In this case, the mapValues method provides a more elegant alternative:

```
def translate(m: Map[String, String]): Map[String, Int] =
  m mapValues (_.length)
```

The following program demonstrates the use of map and the more concise mapValues method. What does it do?

```
val ints = Map("15" -> List(1, 2, 3, 4, 5))
val intsIter1 = ints map { case (k, v) => (k, v.toIterator) }
val intsIter2 = ints mapValues (_.toIterator)

println((intsIter1("15").next, intsIter1("15").next))
println((intsIter2("15").next, intsIter2("15").next))
```

---

[1]An additional example of desugaring a for expression appears in Puzzler 12.

Possibilities

1. Prints:

   ```
   (1,2)
   (1,2)
   ```

2. Prints:

   ```
   (1,1)
   (1,1)
   ```

3. Both `println` statements throw a `NoSuchElementException: next` on empty `iterator`.

4. Prints:

   ```
   (1,2)
   (1,1)
   ```

Explanation

At first sight it appears that both statements should produce the same output, *i.e.*, that the resulting maps should be identical. The first candidate answer, therefore, looks most reasonable. In reality, though, the result is different. The correct answer is number 4:

```scala
scala> println((intsIter1(1).next, intsIter1(1).next))
(1,2)

scala> println((intsIter2(1).next, intsIter2(1).next))
(1,1)
```

In particular, the second invocation of `intsIter2(1).next` produces 1. Could `intsIter2(1)` be iterating over the same element twice? No, the call to next does indeed advance the iterator. How then can the second call to `intsIter2(1).next` produce the same value as the first one? There can

180

only be one explanation: the second call to `intsIter2(1)` returns a *different* iterator than the first. In other words, by some means, a new iterator is created every time a value is retrieved from `intsIter2`.

The documentation for `mapValues` confirms that this is indeed the case. Its description states simply that it "transforms the map by applying a function to every value"—the important detail is hidden in the *returns* part:

> [mapValues returns] a map view[2] that maps every key of this map to `f(this(key))`. The resulting map wraps the original map without copying any elements.

As a result, each retrieval from the wrapped map causes the mapping function, `f`, to be evaluated again, resulting in the creation of a new iterator. This contrasts with the map `intsIter1`, where iterators are created once when the map is transformed, and so every call to `next` is performed on the *same* iterator. This is evident from the following:

```scala
scala> intsIter1(1) eq intsIter1(1)
res0: Boolean = true

scala> intsIter2(1) eq intsIter2(1)
res1: Boolean = false
```

Discussion

The signature of `mapValues` does not indicate that it returns a view:

```scala
def mapValues[C](f: (B) => C): Map[A, C]
```

A more specific return type or more explicit name, such as `mapValuesView`, would make it clearer that the result is actually a view on the original map.

It is also worth pointing out that there are performance implications associated with views, such as those returned by `mapValues`. Since each map value retrieval causes a function application to be performed, repeatedly iterating through such a lazy map can incur considerable overhead if the function is expensive.

---

[2] A *view* is a special kind of collection that lazily applies one or more transformations to an underlying "base" collection.

Usually you can invoke the `force` method on a view to obtain a strict collection, but `collection.immutable.Map`, the type returned by `mapValues`, does not provide a `force` method. To work around this, you have to explicitly convert the map to a view before calling `force`. This produces the expected result:

```
val intsIter2 = ints mapValues (_.toIterator)
val strict = intsIter2.view.force

scala> println(strict(1).next, strict(1).next)
(1,2)
```

The surprising behavior of the code example in this puzzler is one of the reasons immutable data structures and pure functions are strongly favored in idiomatic Scala.

 Familiarize yourself with the differences between views and regular collections, and be aware that `mapValues` returns a view even though it is not obvious from its name or signature.

Puzzler 32

Set the Record Straight

The Scala collections library provides convenience methods, such as toMap, toList, *etc.*, that allow easy conversion between different collection types. The following program shows one of these in action. What does it do?

```scala
val numbers = List("1", "2").toSet() + "3"
println(numbers)
```

Possibilities

1. Prints:

   ```
   Set(1, 2, 3)
   ```

2. Fails to compile.

3. Prints:

   ```
   false3
   ```

4. Prints:

   ```
   123
   ```

Explanation

The candidate answer that looks most probable is perhaps the first one:

```
Set(1, 2, 3)
```

And that would indeed be the correct answer if the first line were:

```
val numbers = List("1", "2").toSet + "3"
```

However, the original program produces an entirely different result.

```
scala> val numbers = List("1", "2").toSet() + "3"
numbers: String = false3
```

The correct answer is number 3. The extra parentheses after `toSet` are the only difference between the two statements. How could this cause the results be so different?

Let's examine closely how the compiler parses the first statement. The method `toSet` on a `List[A]` clearly converts the list to a set, but a careful look at the Scaladoc reveals two important facts:

```
def toSet[B >: A]: Set[B]
```

First, the method itself takes no parameters. Recall that in Scala, if a method is defined without parentheses, it can only be invoked without parentheses:

```
scala> def noParens = "foo"
noParens: String

scala> noParens
res1: String = foo

scala> noParens()
<console>:1: error: not enough arguments for method apply:
  (index: Int)Char in class StringOps.
Unspecified value parameter index.
              noParens()
                      ^
```

Second, the element type of the resulting set can be different than that of the original list. More specifically, the type of the set elements can be a supertype of the list element type.

You could provide the desired element type explicitly:

```scala
scala> List("1", "2").toSet[AnyRef]
res1: scala.collection.immutable.Set[AnyRef] = Set(1, 2)
```

Needless to say, if the type parameter is not provided, the compiler needs
to infer it. Usually, it is fairly obvious—the element type of the resulting
collection is the same as the element type of the source collection:

```scala
scala> List("1", "2").toSet
res2: scala.collection.immutable.Set[String] = Set(1, 2)
```

In this case, however, the additional set of parentheses forces the compiler to
reason differently. Because `toSet` cannot be invoked with parentheses, the
compiler can only interpret the parentheses as an attempt to invoke `apply` on
the *result* of calling `toSet`. Coincidentally, trait `Set[A]` happens to have an
`apply` method, which is equivalent to method `contains`:

```scala
def apply(elem: A): Boolean
```

Tests if some element is contained in this set.

Hence, the compiler treats the invocation of `toSet` with parentheses as:

```scala
List("1", "2").toSet.apply() // apply() == contains()
```

185

But what is the element being tested for in this case? Method `apply` definitely expects an argument (its parameter `elem` does not have a default value) and it looks as if none is being provided. Here a compiler feature called *argument adaptation* comes into play—the compiler adapts the argument list, inserting the `Unit` value, `()`, to match the single parameter specified by the method declaration. You can verify this by compiling the same line of code with the `-Ywarn-adapted-args` option:[1]

```
scala> List("1", "2").toSet.apply()
<console>:8: warning: Adapting argument list by inserting ():
  this is unlikely to be what you want.
        signature: GenSetLike.apply(elem: A): Boolean
  given arguments: <none>
  after adaptation: GenSetLike((): Unit)
              List("1", "2").toSet.apply()
```

As a result of argument adaptation, the final expression is actually:

```
List("1", "2").toSet.apply(())
```

At this point, the compiler must determine whether the set returned by `toSet` contains the `Unit` value. How does that even compile, since the `Unit` value is clearly not a `String`? Recall that the compiler can infer the element type of the resulting set to be *any supertype of* `String`.[2] As illustrated in the Scala type hierarchy,[3] the common supertype of `Unit` and `String` is `Any`. The resulting expression is:

```
List("1", "2").toSet[Any].apply(())
```

This, unsurprisingly, evaluates to `false`, since the `Unit` value is not in the `List`. Thus the actual expression being evaluated is:

false + "3"

Since Scala, like Java, allows `Strings` to be concatenated with any other type, this compiles and results in the string `"false3"`.[4]

---

[1] Starting with Scala 2.11, this behavior has been deprecated and the compiler warning is issued by default. See Puzzler 26 for a more detailed discussion of `-Ywarn-adapted-args` and related compiler options.

[2] See Puzzler 25 for a related discussion.

[3] See Figure 27.1 on page 155.

[4] See Puzzler 36 for a related discussion.

The automatic insertion of the Unit value, (), is actually an unintended consequence of Scala's *auto-tupling* implementation. Auto-tupling allows the compiler to pack multiple method arguments into a tuple where only one argument is expected. For example, given the following method:

```
def tell(o: Any): Unit
```

And an invocation with three arguments:

```
tell(a, b, c)
```

The compiler will pack the three arguments into a single tuple:

```
tell((a, b, c))
```

In case no arguments are given:

```
tell()
```

The compiler will perform a similar transformation:

```
tell(())
```

Here the compiler attempts to insert an "empty tuple," which happens to match the Unit value.[a]

---

[a] See Puzzler 26 for a related discussion.

Discussion

You have already seen that omitting the parentheses after the call to toSet produces the expected result. Note, though, that if you wanted to walk through how the expression is evaluated step-by-step, and what types are inferred along the way, you would find this hard to achieve in the REPL:

```
scala> val list = List("1", "2")
list: List[String] = List(1, 2)
```

```
scala> val set = list.toSet
set: scala.collection.immutable.Set[String] = Set(1, 2)

scala> val result = set()
<console>:9: error: not enough arguments for method apply:
  (elem:String)Boolean in trait GenSetLike.
Unspecified value parameter elem.
        val result = set()
                        ^
```

The last statement here fails to compile because the type widening that turns
Set[String] into Set[Any] does not take place. That is, the element type
of the set has already been inferred as String, so it is no longer possible to
check whether the Unit value, which is clearly not a String, is contained in
the set.

   In the first line of the example program, on the other hand, the type
inferencer is able to infer Any as the element type of the resulting set as it
always examines entire expressions.

   If you want to ensure the original collection type is preserved, you can
use the more general conversion method to, defined on List[A] (or any
Traversable[A], for that matter), with the following signature:

```
def to[Col[_]]: Col[A]
```

Calling this method instead of toSet results in a compiler error:

```
scala> List("1", "2").to[Set]() + "3"
<console>:7: error: not enough arguments for method to:
  (implicit cbf: scala.collection.generic.CanBuildFrom[
  Nothing,String,Set[String]])Set[String].
Unspecified value parameter cbf.
              List("1", "2").to[Set]() + "3"
                                  ^
```

Invoking to correctly (*i.e.*, without parentheses) works as expected:

```
scala> List("1", "2").to[Set] + "3"
res0: scala.collection.immutable.Set[String] = Set(1, 2, 3)
```

Include empty parentheses in method invocations only for side-effecting methods.

Beware of unintended type widening caused by methods on collections that allow the element type of a returned collection to be wider than the original element type.

Puzzler 33

The Devil Is in the Defaults

In many languages, assigning default values to entries in a map involves tedious, boilerplate code:

```scala
import collection.mutable
val accBalances = mutable.Map[String, Int]()

// opening credit is linked to the account holder's name
def getBalance(accHolder: String): Int = {
  if (!(accBalances isDefinedAt accHolder)) {
    accBalances += (accHolder -> accHolder.length)
  }
  accBalances(accHolder)
}
scala> println(getBalance("Alice"))
5
```

Fortunately, you can eliminate this clutter in Scala (and avoid mutable maps as well!) by providing a default function:

```scala
import collection.immutable
val accBalances = immutable.Map[String, Int]() withDefault {
  newCustomer => newCustomer.length }
scala> println(accBalances("Bob"))
3
```

This is a nice, clean way of providing a default value based on the map key. Often, though, the default is not dependent on the key. In that case, Map's withDefaultValue method is a better fit:

```scala
import collection.immutable
val accBalances =
  immutable.Map[String, Int]() withDefaultValue 10

scala> println(accBalances("Bob"))
10
```

In the following example, each account holder starts off with a "thank you for joining" balance of 100 dollars. Accounts are represented in two different ways, as simple balances in accBalances and as balance histories in accBalancesWithHist. Two new customers then cash in on their unexpected gift. What is the result of executing the following code?

```scala
import collection.mutable
import collection.mutable.Buffer

val accBalances: mutable.Map[String, Int] =
  mutable.Map() withDefaultValue 100

def transaction(accHolder: String, amount: Int,
    accounts: mutable.Map[String, Int]) {
  accounts += accHolder -> (accounts(accHolder) + amount)
}

val accBalancesWithHist: mutable.Map[String, Buffer[Int]] =
  mutable.Map() withDefaultValue Buffer(100)

def transactionWithHist(accHolder: String, amount: Int,
    accounts: mutable.Map[String, Buffer[Int]]) {
  val newAmount = accounts(accHolder).head + amount
  accounts += accHolder ->
    (newAmount +=: accounts(accHolder))
}

transaction("Alice", -100, accBalances)
println(accBalances("Alice"))
println(accBalances("Bob"))
```

```
transactionWithHist("Dave", -100, accBalancesWithHist)
println(accBalancesWithHist("Carol").head)
println(accBalancesWithHist("Dave").head)
```

Possibilities

1. Prints:

   ```
   -100
   0
   0
   -100
   ```

2. Prints:

   ```
   0
   100
   0
   100
   ```

3. Prints:

   ```
   0
   100
   100
   0
   ```

4. Prints:

   ```
   0
   100
   0
   0
   ```

Explanation

You may wonder whether updating the map before retrieving any values somehow affects the default, or if the order in which the entries are accessed makes a difference. Adding history to the account representation surely has no impact, though?

Indeed it does. The correct answer is number 4:

```scala
scala> println(accBalances("Alice"))
0

scala> println(accBalances("Bob"))
100

scala> println(accBalancesWithHist("Carol").head)
0

scala> println(accBalancesWithHist("Dave").head)
0
```

So Alice and Bob's account balances are as expected, but Carol and Dave's accounts with history are not behaving as intended. To understand what is going on, compare the actual account objects for Carol and Dave:

```scala
scala> println(accBalancesWithHist("Carol")
          eq accBalancesWithHist("Dave"))
true
```

In other words, once the account history is added, Carol and Dave (and indeed all other account holders) are sharing the same account! The behavior of withDefault may lead you to think that withDefaultValue also acts as a "factory," providing new instances of the default value for each map entry. This is not the case: the same value is used as the default for *all* entries.

Discussion

Since sharing the same value across all map entries can have unexpected consequences, the safest and most predictable approach to providing defaults is to use withDefault, certainly for *mutable* default values. This creates a new instance of the default value for each map entry:

```scala
val accBalancesWithHist2: mutable.Map[String, Buffer[Int]] =
  mutable.Map() withDefault { _ => Buffer(100) }

transactionWithHist("Dave", -100, accBalancesWithHist2)

scala> println(accBalancesWithHist2("Carol").head)
100

scala> println(accBalancesWithHist2("Dave").head)
0
```

If you want to avoid the slight boilerplate of the unused underscore (_) parameter to withDefault's default function, or feel that a method name explicitly mentioning *values* improves readability, you can define your own withDefaultValue method:

```scala
import collection.mutable
import collection.mutable.Buffer
implicit class MapDefaults[A, B](
    val map: mutable.Map[A, B]) extends AnyVal {
  def withNewDefaultValue(d: => B): mutable.Map[A, B] =
    map withDefault { _ => d }
}

...

val accBalancesWithHist: mutable.Map[String, Buffer[Int]] =
  mutable.Map() withNewDefaultValue Buffer(100)

transactionWithHist("Dave", -100, accBalancesWithHist)

scala> println(accBalancesWithHist("Carol").head)
100

scala> println(accBalancesWithHist("Dave").head)
0

scala> println(accBalancesWithHist("Carol")
         eq accBalancesWithHist("Dave"))
false
```

Here, declaring the value passed to withNewDefaultValue as a *by-name parameter*[1,2] causes it to be re-evaluated every time the default function is

---

[1]Odersky, *The Scala Language Specification*, Section 4.6.1. [Ode14]

[2]See Puzzler 23 for a more detailed discussion of by-name parameters.

called. This results in each map entry being assigned a "fresh" instance of the default value.

If the default value is immutable, sharing the same instance across all map entries is not a problem. In fact, if the value is expensive to construct, this will be be cheaper than creating a new instance for each map entry.

Use `Map.withDefaultValue` for immutable defaults only, and `Map.withDefault` otherwise. Be aware that `withDefaultValue` results in the *same* instance of the default value being shared across all map entries.

196

Puzzler 34

The Main Thing

One of the many convenient features of Scala is the ability to put initialization statements directly in a class, trait, or object body, rather than having to define an explicit primary constructor:

```scala
class HelloWorld {
  val msg = "Hello World!"
  println(msg)
}

scala> new HelloWorld
Hello World!
```

Scala leverages this feature to make it equally easy to define programs that can be run from the command line.[1] Instead of having to define a main method, an object can simply inherit from the App trait. The body of the object then automatically becomes the content of the main method, and is executed when the program is run:

```scala
object HelloWorld extends App {
  println("Hello World!")
}

scala> HelloWorld main Array()
Hello World!
```

The following example uses this feature to refactor a simple airport simulator program. In both versions of the simulation, two passengers approach the

---

[1]Odersky, *The Scala Language Specification*, Section 9.5. [Ode14]

check-in desk with a heavy bag, and the desk agent's response is based on how busy the passenger's flight is.

The first version of the simulation defines an explicit main method, the second avoids this boilerplate by extending App. What is the result of executing the following code?

```scala
class AirportDay {
  def tryCheckBag(weight: Int): String =
    "It's not a full flight. Your bag is OK."
}
class StartOfVacation extends AirportDay {
  override def tryCheckBag(weight: Int): String =
    if (weight > 25)
      "Your bag is too heavy. Please repack it."
    else
      "Your bag is OK."
}
def goToCheckIn(bagWeight: Int)(implicit ad: AirportDay) {
  println(s"The agent says: ${ad tryCheckBag bagWeight}")
}
object AirportSim {
  def main(args: Array[String]): Unit = {
    implicit val quietTuesday = new AirportDay
    goToCheckIn(26)
    implicit val busyMonday = new StartOfVacation
    goToCheckIn(26)
  }
}
object AirportSim2 extends App {
  implicit val quietTuesday = new AirportDay
  goToCheckIn(26)
  implicit val busyMonday = new StartOfVacation
  goToCheckIn(26)
}

AirportSim main Array()
AirportSim2 main Array()
```

Possibilities

1. The first airport simulation run prints:

   ```
   The agent says: It's not a full flight. Your bag is OK.
   The agent says: Your bag is too heavy. Please repack it.
   ```

   and the second throws an exception.

2. Prints:

   ```
   The agent says: It's not a full flight. Your bag is OK.
   The agent says: Your bag is too heavy. Please repack it.
   The agent says: It's not a full flight. Your bag is OK.
   The agent says: Your bag is too heavy. Please repack it.
   ```

3. Prints:

   ```
   The agent says: It's not a full flight. Your bag is OK.
   The agent says: Your bag is too heavy. Please repack it.
   The agent says: Your bag is too heavy. Please repack it.
   The agent says: Your bag is too heavy. Please repack it.
   ```

4. Prints:

   ```
   The agent says: Your bag is too heavy. Please repack it.
   The agent says: Your bag is too heavy. Please repack it.
   The agent says: Your bag is too heavy. Please repack it.
   The agent says: Your bag is too heavy. Please repack it.
   ```

Explanation

You may wonder why you do not simply get an "ambiguous implicit values" error in both cases. Or you might conclude that busyMonday takes precedence over quietTuesday, leading the agent to complain about the bag every time. Surely the small change of switching from an explicit main method to inheriting from App does not affect the outcome, though?

In fact, that's exactly what happens. The correct answer is number 1:

```
scala> AirportSim main Array()
The agent says: It's not a full flight. Your bag is OK.
The agent says: Your bag is too heavy. Please repack it.

scala> AirportSim2 main Array()
java.lang.NullPointerException
  at .goToCheckIn(<console>:9)
  ...
  at AirportSim2$.main(<console>:10)
  ...
```

A NullPointerException? Where is that coming from? To understand what is happening here, take a look at what's going on in AirportSim, the first airport simulation.

Both invocations of goToCheckIn(26) in AirportSim.main require an implicit AirportDay. When goToCheckIn is first called, there is only one candidate in scope, quietTuesday, as it is the only implicit that has been declared at this point in the code. The desk agent, therefore, is lenient and lets the traveler through.

By the time goToCheckIn is called again, a *second* suitable implicit, busyMonday, has been declared and is thus in scope. Now, the compiler needs to determine which implicit is most specific[2] by applying the rules of static overloading resolution.[3]

According to these rules, StartOfVacation is indeed more specific as it inherits from AirportDay, so there is no "ambiguous implicit values" error and the unlucky traveler is told to repack.[4]

What, then, differs in the case of AirportSim2? Well, even though the language specification describes App as "a special class whose body acts as a main method,"[5] its body is not actually a method—it is a constructor. So the implicit vals declared here are not local variables, they are *object members*.[6]

This means that *both* implicits are in scope everywhere in the object body. Specifically, busyMonday is also applicable at the moment of the *first* call to goToCheckIn in AirportSim2. As the most specific implicit in scope, it is chosen by the compiler.

---

[2]Odersky, *The Scala Language Specification*, Section 7.2. [Ode14]
[3]Odersky, *The Scala Language Specification*, Section 6.26.3. [Ode14]
[4]See Puzzler 29 for a related discussion.
[5]Odersky, *The Scala Language Specification*, Section 9.5. [Ode14]
[6]Odersky, *The Scala Language Specification*, Section 5.1.3. and 5.4. [Ode14]

How does the `NullPointerException` come about? This, it turns out, is the result of the order of the statements in the constructor. The position of the implicit `val` declarations does not indicate when the `val`s come into scope, but it *does* determine when the values are actually initialized. According to the language specification, the initialization statements in the body of `AirportSim2` are indeed executed in order.[7]

This means that busyMonday—the most specific implicit in scope—*has not been initialized yet* when it is passed to the first call to `goToCheckIn(26)` in `AirportSim2`. It therefore has the default value for its type: `null`. When `goToCheckIn` tries to invoke it, the observed `NullPointerException` results.

Discussion

The fact that values declared in a constructor are visible throughout the class or object and can be referenced *before* they are initialized applies to "regular" `val`s and `var`s too, and to classes as well as objects:

```
class HelloWorld {
  println(message)
  val message = "Hello World!"
}

scala> new HelloWorld
null
```

Luckily, the compiler can spot these references and will emit an appropriate warning:

```
scala> class HelloWorld {
         println(message)
         val message = "Hello World!"
       }
<console>:8: warning: Reference to uninitialized value
  message
         println(message)
                 ^
```

---

[7] Odersky, *The Scala Language Specification*, Section 5.1. [Ode14]

The same, likely unexpected, change in behavior occurs when moving expressions from an auxiliary constructor of a class to the primary constructor. Auxiliary constructors, even though they are also constructors, behave like AirportSim's main method. Values declared in an auxiliary constructor are treated as local variables, and the constructor expression is evaluated as if it were a function:[8]

```scala
class AirportSimAuxiliaryCons {
  def this(weight: Int) {
    this()
    implicit val quietTuesday = new AirportDay
    goToCheckIn(weight)

    implicit val busyMonday = new StartOfVacation
    goToCheckIn(weight)
  }
}

scala> new AirportSimAuxiliaryCons(26)
The agent says: It's not a full flight. Your bag is OK.
The agent says: Your bag is too heavy. Please repack it.
```

The same implicit values, when declared in the primary constructor, are now class members as in the case of AirportSim2. As a result, they are both in scope also for the first call to goToCheckIn, leading to the same NullPointerException observed earlier:

```scala
class AirportSimPrimaryCons(weight: Int) {
  implicit val quietTuesday = new AirportDay
  goToCheckIn(weight)

  implicit val busyMonday = new StartOfVacation
  goToCheckIn(weight)
}

scala> new AirportSimPrimaryCons(26)
java.lang.NullPointerException
  at .goToCheckIn(<console>:9)
  ...
```

---

[8]Odersky, *The Scala Language Specification*, Section 5.3.1. [Ode14]

202

Unlike local variables in a method, which are not in scope until they are declared, variables declared at the top level of a class or object body are *members*, which are in scope throughout the class or object. They remain uninitialized until the line in the code that declares them is reached.

Watch for compiler warnings that indicate references to uninitialized variables. Verify that the reference really is intentional, and that your code will correctly handle the (uninitialized) default value.

Puzzler 35

A Listful of Dollars

A convenient feature that allows Scala to cater to different coding styles is that you can often substitute curly braces for parentheses:

```scala
scala> (1 to 3).foreach(r =>
          print("%.5f ".format(math.Pi * r * r)))
3.14159 12.56637 28.27433

scala> (1 to 3) foreach { r =>
          print("%.5f ".format(math.Pi * r * r)) }
3.14159 12.56637 28.27433
```

Scala also provides type aliases, which allows you to give more convenient names to nontrivial types and domain-specific names to general types:

```scala
// letters -> terms and the pages on which they appear
type BookIndex = Map[Char, Map[String, Seq[Int]]]

type Fahrenheit = Int
type Celsius = Int
// compare with 'def toFahrenheit(celsius: Int): Int'
def toFahrenheit(c: Celsius): Fahrenheit
```

The following program uses both of these features. What does it do?

```scala
type Dollar = Int
final val Dollar: Dollar = 1
val x: List[Dollar] = List(1, 2, 3)

println(x map { x: Int => Dollar })
println(x.map(x: Int => Dollar))
```

Possibilities

1. Prints:

   ```
   List(1, 2, 3)
   List(1, 2, 3)
   ```

2. Prints:

   ```
   List(1, 1, 1)
   List(1, 1, 1)
   ```

3. The first `println` statement prints:

   ```
   List(1, 1, 1)
   ```

   and the second one throws an exception.

4. The first `println` statement prints:

   ```
   List(1, 2, 3)
   ```

   and the second one fails to compile.

Explanation

You may wonder whether both statements compile, but if they do, surely
it makes no difference whether you use curly braces or parentheses here.
Actually, it does—the correct answer is number 3:

```
scala> println(x map { x: Int => Dollar })
List(1, 1, 1)

scala> println(x.map(x: Int => Dollar))
java.lang.IndexOutOfBoundsException: 3
    ...
```

The key point is that an anonymous function can be parsed differently if it is passed in a *block expression*,[1] as opposed to being passed directly.[2] To understand how this results in the observed behavior, consider two different ways of interpreting the function expression:

```
x: Int => Dollar
```

One way to see this is as a function that takes an `Int` and returns the value `Dollar`, *i.e.*, the constant value 1. In other words, you might conclude that x is a *parameter*:

```
(x: Int) => Dollar
```

Although it is never incorrect to place parentheses around parameter lists for anonymous functions, they can be omitted in certain cases. Specifically, parentheses are not required if a function takes one parameter and no type is given, as in x => Dollar. If a type is specified for the parameter, you can omit the parentheses only if the anonymous function appears as a block. This is precisely what is going on in the first `println` statement:

```
println(x map { x: Int => Dollar })
```

This statement is equivalent to the following, shorter, form:

```
println(x map { freshName => 1 })
```

Not surprisingly, the result is a list of 1 values:

```
scala> println(x map { x: Int => Dollar })
List(1, 1, 1)
```

Note that the two occurrences of x in this expression have different meanings: the first x refers to the list, while the second one represents a parameter of the function passed to map.

In the case of the second `println` statement, the anonymous function is not passed as a block expression:

```
println(x.map(x: Int => Dollar))
```

---

[1]Odersky, *The Scala Language Specification*, Section 6.23. [Ode14]
[2]Anonymous functions passed in block expressions are also discussed in Puzzler 1.

Given that the parentheses around the parameter, x: Int, are omitted and the expression x: Int => Dollar is not inside a block, you might wonder how it even compiles. The answer is that this function expression can be read in a different way, by treating the type declaration as a type ascription to the entire expression. In other words, the expression x: Int => Dollar is parsed as x: (Int => Dollar), with x a function of type Int => Dollar, and Dollar a type alias for Int.

This means that both occurrences of x in the second println statement refer to the *same* value, the list x. This is only possible because Scala's List is also a Function1, which maps list indices to elements in the list. List x, a List[Dollar], is therefore a function from Int to Dollar, the type expected by map. The statement thus compiles without errors.

At runtime, consequently, the second println statement uses each value in the list as an index back into itself. More specifically, it tries to map List(1, 2, 3) to List(x(1), x(2), x(3)). Because list x only has three elements, this will work until passing the last index value, 3, results in the observed IndexOutOfBoundException.

Discussion

To achieve the same result when passing the anonymous function directly as when passing a block expression, you need to enclose the parameter in parentheses:

```
scala> println(x.map((x: Int) => Dollar))
List(1, 1, 1)
```

If the parameter is untyped, both println statements behave the same way:

```
scala> println(x map { x => Dollar })
List(1, 1, 1)

scala> println(x.map(x => Dollar))
List(1, 1, 1)
```

While you can pass anonymous functions whose body consists of a single expression directly or as a block, a block expression is required in the following two situations:

```
// multiple statements in function body
Seq(1, 2, 3) map { e =>
  val i = e + 1
  i * 2
}
// using case clauses
Seq(1, 2, 3) map {
  case e if e % 2 == 0 => e + 2
  case e => e + 1
}
```

 Be aware that passing an anonymous function
in curly braces actually creates a block.
Anonymous functions passed in a block can be
parsed differently than when passed directly.

If you are passing an anonymous,
single-parameter function in parentheses,
make sure you enclose the parameter in
parentheses if it has a type annotation.

Puzzler 36

Size It Up

One of the goals of the Scala collections is to make common operations, such as concatenating two collections, concise and easy to read. To that end, the collection types support a number of operators, such as ++ and +:, allowing you to write expressions "naturally" and avoid method names such as concat or prepend.

The following code example uses one of these operations to determine how many items are in a young Scala enthusiast's lunchbox. In order to ensure an at least moderately healthy diet, we sneak an apple into the lunchbox as well.

Our Scala enthusiast has the peculiar habit of never taking more than *one* of each item, so the code starts out by assuming that lunchboxes are sets. Realizing that this is something of a special case, we update the code to allow arbitrary selections of items and count the number of items in the "apple-reinforced" lunchbox, using the original function that assumes lunchboxes are sets and the updated version that allows for arbitrary collections. What is the result of executing the following code?

```scala
import collection.mutable

def howManyItems(lunchbox: mutable.Set[String],
  itemToAdd: String): Int = (lunchbox + itemToAdd).size

def howManyItemsRefac(lunchbox: mutable.Iterable[String],
  itemToAdd: String): Int = (lunchbox + itemToAdd).size

val lunchbox =
  mutable.Set("chocolate bar", "orange juice", "sandwich")
```

```
println(howManyItems(lunchbox, "apple"))
println(howManyItemsRefac(lunchbox, "apple"))
println(lunchbox.size)
```

Possibilities

1. Prints:

    ```
    4
    5
    5
    ```

2. Prints:

    ```
    4
    4
    3
    ```

3. Prints:

    ```
    4
    4
    4
    ```

4. Prints:

    ```
    4
    47
    3
    ```

Explanation

You may wonder whether treating the lunchbox as an `Iterable`, as in the case of howManyItemsRefac, somehow allows the addition of a second apple. Or you may suspect that adding an apple creates a *new* lunchbox, rather than modifying the lunchbox passed to the counting functions, which would result in 4, 4, and 3 being printed.

As it happens, that is close, but not quite the case. The correct answer is number 4:

```scala
scala> println(howManyItems(lunchbox, "apple"))
4
scala> println(howManyItemsRefac(lunchbox, "apple"))
47
scala> println(lunchbox.size)
3
```

What is happening here? The first point to observe is that the suspicion that the lunchbox passed to the counting function is not actually modified is correct. The + method on both mutable and immutable `Sets` creates a *new* set, consisting of the elements of the original set together with the argument passed. The method on a mutable set that actually *modifies* the set is +=. So howManyItems returns the size of a new lunchbox with an additional apple, but does not actually add the apple to the lunchbox passed in. This explains why the first `println` statement outputs 4 but the final one prints 3.

Where do the 47 lunchbox items found by howManyItemsRefac come from, then? Well, it so happens that + is not actually a method supported by `Iterable`, but it *is* Scala's string concatenation operator. And `itemToAdd` is indeed a string.

Of course, `lunchbox` is *not* a string, so the Scala compiler starts looking for an applicable implicit conversion[1] to help. And it finds one, in the form of `Predef.any2stringadd`.[2] As its name applies, this default implicit can convert any object to a `String` so it can be concatenated with another string.

The body of the function howManyItemsRefac is, essentially:

```scala
Predef.any2stringadd(lunchbox).+(itemToAdd).size
```

---

[1] Odersky, *The Scala Language Specification*, Section 6.26. [Ode14]
[2] See Puzzler 30 for a related discussion of implicit resolution.

This means that howManyItemsRefac does not return the number of items in the lunchbox after adding an apple, but rather the length of the string lunchbox.toString + "apple":

```scala
def howManyItemsDebug(lunchbox: mutable.Iterable[String],
    itemToAdd: String): Int = {
  val concatenatedStrings = lunchbox.toString + itemToAdd
  println(s"DEBUG: ${concatenatedStrings}")
  concatenatedStrings.size
}

scala> println(howManyItemsDebug(lunchbox, "apple"))
DEBUG: Set(orange juice, sandwich, chocolate bar)apple
47
```

Discussion

The main reason any2stringadd exists is for consistency with Java. Recall that Java also supports concatenation of any object with a string. This is convenient for quick debugging statements:

```scala
case class Pet(name: String, species: String)
println(Pet("garfield", "cat") + " is my pet")
```

Due to any2stringadd's penchant for causing confusion by appearing in unexpected places in your code, there are frequent calls for it to be removed. This is likely to happen in future, although not necessarily in the short term.

Luckily, you can disable this or indeed any other default implicit in your programs, by using an *import selector*[3] to "rename" the implicits in question to the wildcard symbol _. This makes them effectively inaccessible. These import statements must be the *first* lines in your source file.

Disabling implicits in the REPL is possible using the :paste -raw command, which treats the subsequent input as a Scala file, rather than a script:

```scala
scala> :paste -raw
// Entering paste mode (ctrl-D to finish)
```

---

[3]Odersky, *The Scala Language Specification*, Section 4.7. [Ode14]

214

```
import Predef.{any2stringadd => _, _}
object SizeItUp {
  import collection.mutable
  def howManyItemsRefac(lunchbox: mutable.Iterable[String],
    itemToAdd: String): Int = (lunchbox + itemToAdd).size
}
// Exiting paste mode, now interpreting.
<pastie>:5: error: value + is not a member of
  scala.collection.mutable.Iterable[String]
    itemToAdd: String): Int = (lunchbox + itemToAdd).size
                                        ^
```

Here, the second wildcard (_) in import Predef.{any2stringadd => _, _}
ensures that all *other* members of Predef are still imported.

An easier, if less elegant, way of disabling an implicit conversion is to
deliberately cause an "ambiguous implicit values" clash. In order for this to
work, you need to introduce not one, but *two* new conversions. If you define
only one implicit, it will be more specific than the conversion in Predef
you want to disable and will be chosen instead, rather than producing the
intended conflict:

```
object NoAny2StringAdd {
  implicit val disableAny2stringadd1 = (_: Any) => ""
  implicit val disableAny2stringadd2 = (_: Any) => ""
}
import collection.mutable
import NoAny2StringAdd._

scala> def howManyItemsRefac(
          lunchbox: mutable.Iterable[String],
          itemToAdd: String): Int =
       (lunchbox + itemToAdd).size
<console>:13: error: type mismatch;
 found    : lunchbox.type (with underlying type
   scala.collection.mutable.Iterable[String])
 required: ?{def +(x$1: ? >: String): ?}
Note that implicit conversions are not applicable
  because they are ambiguous:
  both value disableAny2stringadd1 in object NoAny2StringAdd
```

215

```
    of type => Any => String
  and value disableAny2stringadd2 in object NoAny2StringAdd
    of type => Any => String
  are possible conversion functions from lunchbox.type to
    ?{def +(x$1: ? >: String): ?}
          (lunchbox + itemToAdd).size
                    ^
```

A more straightforward way of preventing unintended string concatenations is to explicitly specify the expected type of collection operations:

```
scala> def howManyItemsRefac(
            lunchbox: mutable.Iterable[String],
            itemToAdd: String): Int = {
          val healthierLunchbox: mutable.Iterable[String] =
            lunchbox + itemToAdd
          healthierLunchbox.size
        }
  <console>:10: error: type mismatch;
   found    : String
   required: scala.collection.mutable.Iterable[String]
            lunchbox + itemToAdd
                    ^
```

Using an intermediate val in this way should not incur any performance penalty: the compiler will generally be able to optimize away the intermediate value.

Be aware that the Scala compiler can always fall back to treating the + operator as string concatenation if the argument is a string. If the expression is not intended to return a String, specify the expected result type explicitly. You can disable Predef.any2stringadd in your program to prevent the implicit conversion of any object to a string.

Bibliography

[Dou]   "(Double.NaN min 0.0) yields 0.0, should be NaN." *Scala Programming Language / SI-5104*. Available on the web at https://issues.scala-lang.org/browse/SI-5104 (accessed November 17, 2014).

[EPF]   EPFL. *Scala Standard Library, Scaladoc Documentation*. Available on the web at http://www.scala-lang.org/api/current/ (accessed November 17, 2014).

[Fow99] Fowler, Martin. *Refactoring: Improving the Design of Existing Code*. Addison-Wesley, first edition, 1999.

[Gle11] Gleichmann, Mario. "Functional Scala: Turning Methods into Functions." January 2011. Available on the web at http://gleichmann.wordpress.com/2011/01/09/functional-scala-turning-methods-into-functions/ (accessed November 17, 2014).

[Gri10] Griffith, Dave. "Purpose of 'return' statement in Scala?" September 2010. Available on the web at http://stackoverflow.com/a/3771243/391960 (accessed November 17, 2014).

[Har]   Harrah, Mark. "Value Classes and Universal Traits." Available on the web at http://docs.scala-lang.org/overviews/core/value-classes.html (accessed November 17, 2014).

[Lin13] Lindholm, Tim, Frank Yellin, Gilad Bracha, and Alex Buckley. *The Java Virtual Machine Specification, Java SE7 Edition*. February 2013. Available on the web at http://docs.oracle.com/javase/specs/jvms/se7/html/ (accessed November 17, 2014).

[Mat12] Mathias. "The Magnet Pattern." December 2012. Available on the web at http://spray.io/blog/2012-12-13-the-magnet-pattern/ (accessed November 17, 2014).

[Odea] Odersky, Martin and Lex Spoon. "Collections: Views." Available on the web at http://docs.scala-lang.org/overviews/collections/views.html (accessed November 17, 2014).

[Odeb] Odersky, Martin, Lex Spoon, and Bill Venners. "Programming in Scala, Glossary." Available on the web at http://docs.scala-lang.org/glossary/#uniform_access_principle (accessed November 17, 2014).

[Ode10] Odersky, Martin, Lex Spoon, and Bill Venners. *Programming in Scala*. Artima, second edition, 2010.

[Ode14] Odersky, Martin. *The Scala Language Specification, Version 2.8*. EPFL, January 2014. Available on the web at http://www.scala-lang.org/docu/files/ScalaReference.pdf (accessed November 17, 2014).

[Ora] Oracle. *Java Platform, Standard Edition 8 API Specification*. Available on the web at https://docs.oracle.com/javase/8/docs/api/index.html (accessed November 17, 2014).

[Sob10] Sobral, Daniel. "Implicit tricks – the Type Class pattern." June 2010. Available on the web at http://dcsobral.blogspot.com/2010/06/implicit-tricks-type-class-pattern.html (accessed November 17, 2014).

[Spi] Spiewak, Daniel and David Copeland. *Scala Style Guide*. EPFL. Available on the web at http://docs.scala-lang.org/style/ (accessed November 17, 2014).

[Sue] Suereth, Josh. "Implicit Classes." Available on the web at http://docs.scala-lang.org/overviews/core/implicit-classes.html (accessed November 17, 2014).

218

[Why]   "Why is my abstract or overridden val Article?" Available on
           the web at http://docs.scala-lang.org/tutorials/FAQ/initialization-
           order.html (accessed November 17, 2014).

[Zau10a]   Zaugg, Jason.   "In Scala, why can't I partially ap-
           ply a function without explicitly specifying its argument
           types?"   March 2010.   Available on the web at
           http://stackoverflow.com/a/2394063/391960 (accessed November
           17, 2014).

[Zau10b]   Zaugg,   Jason.   "Why   'avoid   method   overload-
           ing'?"   March 2010.   Available on the web at
           http://stackoverflow.com/questions/2510108/why-avoid-method-
           overloading/#2512001 (accessed November 17, 2014).

About the Authors

Andrew Phillips

Specializing in concurrency and high-performance applications, Andrew developed large-scale systems while working for a succession of multinational companies. A long-standing open-source developer and community member, he worked on Multiverse, the STM implementation originally used in Akka; contributes to Apache jclouds, the leading Java cloud library; and co-maintains the Scala Puzzlers website. He regularly writes for developer sites and speaks at conferences and meetups.

Andrew studied Artificial Intelligence and Mathematics at the University of Edinburgh and maintains a keen interest in machine learning, quantum computation, and computational neuroscience.

Nermin Šerifović

Nermin Šerifović has more than ten years of experience developing enterprise software applications using Java technologies. For most of his career, he has focused on building backend platforms. Nermin has been a Scala enthusiast since 2009, practicing it professionally since 2011. He is an instructor at Harvard Extension School, where he co-teaches 'Concurrent Programming in Scala' course and has also given talks at various conferences.

An active Scala community member, Nermin organized the Boston Area Scala Enthusiasts user group and was part of the Northeast Scala Symposium founding team. He is a co-creator of the Scala Puzzlers website.

Nermin holds an M.Eng in Computer Science from Cornell University and his areas of interest include distributed systems along with concurrent, reactive, and functional programming.

Subject Index

Index

Index

construct . . . , 81
Reference to uninitialized value
. . . , 54, 74, 201
value . . . does nothing other
than call itself recursively,
75
concise code, 3, 6, 13, 31, 37, 79
constant values, 10, 34
pattern matching, 10, 11
stable identifiers, 10
uppercase variable names, 12
vals, 12
constructors, 21, 26, 50, 200
arguments, 16, 133–135
auxiliary, 202
body, 15, 17, 21
parameters, 15
primary, 202
no-arg, 134
statements, order of, 201
superclass, 17
trait, 17
control flow, 81
nested functions, 80
control structures, 79
convenience methods
toSet, 183
curly braces
block expressions, 5
early field definitions, 26
parentheses, instead of, 95,
131–135, 205
curried definitions, 34, 35, 147
curried functions, 100, 147
curried invocations, 35
curried parameters, 147
currying, 91–96
cyclic definitions, 48, 51, 54
cyclic dependencies, 47, 54
cyclic references, 24

D

data structures

immutable, 182
debugging statement, 3
declaration order, 49, 53, 54
default arguments, 91–96, 109–113
at runtime
invoking default methods,
112
with named parameters, 91
default implicits, 169
default initial values, 21, 22, 50, 53,
160, 161
default methods, 111
default parameter values, 91
default values, 111, 191–196
mutable, 194
uninitialized, 75, 202
deferring
evaluations, 85
desugar, 43, 46
for comprehensions, 43, 45
for loop, 69
generators, 45
guards, 46
map, 44
Double class
in default initial values, 22

E

eager evaluations, 85
eager vals, 24
early field definitions, 16, 17
curly braces, 26
early initializers, 25
elegant approach
using lazy vals, 66
elegant syntax, 43
empty argument list, 134
endless loop, 48–50, 52, 54, 175, 177
equals method
behavior unaffected, 58
compiler-generated overridden
implementation, 59

runtime error
    scala.MatchError: ..., 144
runtime exceptions, 9, 12, 47, 52, 64
    Java
        IllegalStateException: No
            match available ..., 117
        IndexOutOfBoundsExcep-
            tion: ..., 38,
            40
        NullPointerException: ...,
            163, 200, 202
        StackOverflowError: ..., 51,
            175
        StringIndexOutOfBoundsEx-
            ception: ...,
            120
    Java.NullPointerException, 74
    Scala
        MatchError: ..., 44, 46
        NonLocalReturnControl: ...,
            81
        UninitializedFieldError: ...,
            22
runtime type, 112

S

Scala collections library, 27–30
    methods
        concat, 211
        prepend, 211
        toSet, 183
Scala language
    best practices, 12
    class hierarchy diagram, 155
    features
        auto-tupling, 149
        curly braces, 131–135
    good practices, 60, 157, 173
    strengths
        interoperability with Java,
            153
Scala style, 40, 60, 157, 173, 182,
    185

idiomatic, 79, 88
immutability, 88
Scala's null-safe versions
    == (equals), 163
    ## (hashCode), 163, 164
LowPriorityImplicits class, 169
Scaladoc, 58n, 93n, 184, 189
self-references, 74, 75
    avoiding, 76
    in variable definitions, 76
Seq trait
    in Scala collections library, 27,
        37, 40, 43–46
    methods
        map, 43–46
Set trait
    in Scala collections library,
        27–30
    methods
        map, 29
        size, 29
Short class
    in default initial values, 22
side effects, 84, 88, 89, 134
    class MatchIterator in class
        Regex, 117
singleton, 52
size method
    on class List, 29
    on trait Iterable, 27, 29, 30
    on trait Set, 29
SortedSet trait
    iteration order
        determined by elements, 70
sorting, 141
    on NaN, 139
sorting algorithms
    mirroring compareTo method
        on class Double, in Java, 141
    NaN, handling of, 141
    stableSort method, 139
stable identifiers